“Who doesn’t ye
and expectatio
anywhere else but in Christ, *Sanctuary* is a helpful guide for the restless heart.”

Kristen Wetherell, Author, *Humble Moms* and *Fight Your Fears*; Co-author, *Hope When It Hurts*

“This book is right on time! We are in desperate need of sanctuary. Denise invites us into a deeply restful rhythm of grace—that we might re-emerge with peace and purpose as lights for Christ.”

Wendy Speake, Author, *The 40-Day Sugar Fast* and *The 40-Day Feast*

“*Sanctuary* offers us an opportunity to spend 31 days reflecting deeply on our relationships with the digital world, our physical community, and our heavenly Father. Denise takes an honest and gracious devotional look at topics including identity, choice, competition, simplicity, silence, purpose, and more.”

Michelle Van Loon, Author, *Translating Your Past*

“We live in unprecedented times of innovation. Yet, in this hyper-connected world, our souls are often torn between the good that technology provides and the ever-growing call to do and be more. In *Sanctuary*, Denise provides biblical perspective for how to live the abundant, peace-filled life God promises.”

Katie Orr, Bible teacher; Author, *FOCUSed 15 Bible Studies* and *Secrets of the Happy Soul*

"Powerfully yet gently, Denise exposes the noise that fills our lives and leads us on a journey towards the peace that God alone gives. This book will do your heart good."

Linda Allcock, Author, *Head, Heart, Hands* and *Deeper Still*

"*Sanctuary* brings an important challenge: to be countercultural, resting in the identity that God, not society, gives us. Denise wisely and winsomely encourages her readers to find their ultimate sanctuary in God's presence through his word. I can think of no better way to start each day."

Shelly Wildman, Speaker; Author, *First Ask Why*

"Denise reminds us of our deep need for quiet and tranquility in this noisy, overwhelming world. With biblically solid words filled with wisdom, let her walk you through a 31-day journey of hope, with wise strategies to help you unplug and dive deep into the rest and stillness found only in Christ."

Kate Battistelli, Author, *The God Dare* and *Growing Great Kids*

"All devotionals are not created equal, and *Sanctuary* is one of those that will linger with you long after you've put it down, in all the ways that make a difference, now and forever. No box-checking here: simply a lovely guide to help you silence the clamor of a noisy world."

Robin Dance, Life Plan Advisor; Speaker; Author, *For All Who Wander* and *For All Who Wander The Journey Guide*

DENISE J. HUGHES

sanctuary

CULTIVATING A QUIET HEART IN A NOISY AND DEMANDING WORLD

Sanctuary

Published by:
The Good Book Company

thegoodbook COMPANY

thegoodbook.com | thegoodbook.co.uk
thegoodbook.com.au | thegoodbook.co.nz | thegoodbook.co.in

ISBN: 9781784988180 | Printed in Turkey

Cover design by Jennifer Phelps | Art Direction and design by André Parker

Contents

Introduction

SEARCHING FOR SANCTUARY

"But we encourage you, brothers and sisters … to seek to lead a quiet life."

1 Thessalonians 4:10-11

My phone chimed with an all-too-familiar tune. Another message awaited me. I reached for it, but before I could listen, another one came in. That made 18 so far that day, and it was only 10:45 in the morning. Begrudgingly, I listened to the voice-recorded messages, which were part of a larger group chat.

"Check it, girls. These fab magnetic eyelashes are ON SALE!"

"Oh, I love those!"

The messages continued to roll in as a slow sigh escaped my lips. I didn't haven't time for silly convos about fake eyelashes. I had a deadline to meet before picking up my kids from school and starting my afternoon job as their chauffeur. How did I even get added to this group chat in the first place? Oh, yeah. It had started as a work-related thread. We all worked remotely for the same company, and rather than typing out whole words in emails, several of the staff thought voice messages via this new app would be faster and easier. Soon, the convenience of leaving voice messages morphed into sending funny jokes or helpful tips about the latest online sales. If someone's favorite leggings or magnetic eyelashes were on sale, they figured the rest of us were dying to know about it.

I enjoyed my work and my colleagues, and I appreciated the technological advances that made remote work possible. But it came with a downside, too. The noise had become a constant backdrop because everyone preferred a different mode of communication. While some preferred voice messages through an app, others preferred texts, or emails, or one of the hundred-plus channels in Slack.

With so many messages coming at me day and night, it felt impossible to concentrate on the actual work in front of me. Perhaps the quirky GIFs and memes were meant to lighten the mood, but when your workload is already too heavy, the extra messages become too much. I wanted to run away from the noise. I wanted a place of quiet where I could focus and do my work—a place where I could hear myself think.

But noise is everywhere. When reading an online article, advertisements pop up, telling us how our lives will be so much better if we purchase their magical product for $19.99. When trying to read the news, we're bombarded with outrage. And when we log off of our computers, the noise follows us: The too-loud music in the grocery store. The turned-up television in the doctor's waiting room. And the talk-to-you pumps at the gas station, where a video starts the moment we begin filling our cars with fuel.

Silencing the Noise

The world continues to grow louder every day. This is happening so incrementally that we may not notice it, or if we do, we may shrug it off as no big deal. But somewhere along the way, it has begun to affect us. For some, the added stimulation might be energizing, but for others, the noise takes a toll. At first, it was hard to describe, but slowly, many of us noticed the way noise impacts us. When we're surrounded by noise, it's as if our souls have a slow leak and we can feel our energy ebbing away.

Do you feel tired, and you can't quite pinpoint the source of your exhaustion? Has your social-media feed sometimes felt anything but social? Are you weary from all the conflict and outrage that pervades Twitter threads and other online formats? Do you ever experience a sense of restlessness deep within you? Do you sometimes wish you could log off forever?

A few years ago, I would have answered, "Yes, to all of the above!" In many ways, though, it was part of my job to be online, but it left me just plain tired. Like so many of the women I talked to, I wanted something more than Facebook likes or Instagram hearts. I was ready for something deeper than an online high-five or another blue thumbs-up. I was eager to eliminate the noise from my life, but it had become so ubiquitous that I hardly knew how to escape it.

For a while I dreamed of escaping to a little cabin on a lake in Minnesota. A cabin without internet access. Where there's only earth and sky, water and trees. Where the air is clear and you can actually hear the rustling of leaves. But I don't have an internet-free cabin close to the Canadian border. For the past two-and-a-half decades, I have lived 20 miles from downtown Los Angeles, planted amid the massive urban-to-suburban sprawl. This meant I needed to be intentional about creating spaces of quiet—not only in my physical environment but in my heart as well—because it's really the heart that drives us.

And that's the thing I've noticed most: as much as I want to point to the noise around me, the real noise is inside of me, like a restlessness I can't shake or a gnawing feeling that won't go away. And since it's impossible to run away from myself, the amped-up noise around me serves as a digital distraction, a temporary salve. But in my most honest moments, I long for sanctuary.

Finding Sanctuary

In the classic story, *The Hunchback of Notre-Dame*, the gypsy Esmeralda runs into a cathedral to escape the dark clutches of those chasing her, and she cries, "Sanctuary!" While this story is the stuff of fiction, the need to find sanctuary has historical precedent. In Old Testament times, God arranged for designated cities in the promised land to be "sanctuary cities": places of refuge, where an accused person could flee for safety until a fair trial could be held (Numbers 35:9-34). This same idea has lived on in various forms throughout the centuries, as with modern-day embassies around the world. And even though the New Testament never equates the church with a physical building, in many churches, the word *sanctuary* is still used to describe the main room where people gather.

For too long I felt a little like Esmeralda, wanting to cry, "Sanctuary!" in response to the noise around me. But running away to a cathedral in France wasn't a realistic option, so I had to learn how to cultivate a quiet sanctuary of the heart while living in one of the largest—and loudest—metropolitan areas in the world.

Given the noise that has become so prevalent in our cultural climate, many of us are longing for a simpler and more peaceful way to live. We need a vision for cultivating a quiet sanctuary of the heart, and Paul encapsulates this vision succinctly when he says, "Seek to lead a quiet life" (1 Thessalonians 4:11). As we delve more into the context, we'll discover that a quiet life doesn't mean a life of silence; it means…

- a life free from constant noise and hustle.
- a life defined by purpose rather than ambition.
- a life of "minding your own business," (v 11) and free from comparison.
- a life of focus, "working with our own hands," (v 11) instead of distraction.
- a life characterized by a quiet confidence and a steady peace.
- a life of loving others (v 10) and winning their respect (v 12).

Paul's admonition to lead a quiet life was not only countercultural then; it's still countercultural today. His instructions to believers, both then and now, have never been more needed. In the coming pages we'll learn how, as we embrace a quiet life, something shifts as noise and hurry no longer define us. We are freed to love God and others more fully and more deeply.

Cultivating a quiet life isn't a trend or a brand; it's a way of life that emanates from a soul committed to becoming more like Christ. That's what this book is about: identifying both the external and internal noise that is, in fact, draining us and then reimagining a different way to engage with the world with God's love without wanting to flee to a remote island.

This book is for those who…

- long for quieter spaces that allow for thoughtful reflections and honest conversations.
- desire a deeper quality of life beyond the online culture of noise, outrage, and self-promotion.

- recognize the importance of investing in physical places and nondigital activities.
- want to glean the best the internet has to offer while staying rooted in real-life relationships.
- hope to write a different script for their future by looking to Christ as their sanctuary.

In short, this book is for anyone who is tired of all the noise in our world.

It's possible to live in a digitally driven world without it driving us crazy. It's possible to work in an overconnected environment without it leaving us depleted and exhausted. It's possible to embrace the positives of modern technology without it overrunning our lives. It's possible to find peace and hope and laughter and rest in a world that thrives on conflict and outrage. It's possible to flourish in an urban or suburban context while cultivating a sanctuary of quiet in both your heart and your home. It's possible to live in such a way that others take notice of the difference they see in you and then want what you have found.

That's what I'm inviting you to do with me now.

Together, we are about to embark on a 31-day journey to discover what it means—and what it looks like in very practical ways—to cultivate a quiet life while also engaging with the world around us. Together, we will become women with vision, women with passion, and women who have a heart for championing other women.

Are you ready for something deeper than digital connection? Something real, something lasting?

Are you ready to move through your days with a quiet sense of purpose, rather than following the cultural rigmarole that comes with the status quo?

Cultivating a quiet life
isn't a trend or a brand;
it's a way of life that
emanates from a soul
committed to becoming
more like Christ.

This book doesn't promise a secret ingredient or a radical innovation. Instead, these pages explore the ordinary ways that faithful believers have been growing in quiet grace for millennia.

The life of peace and purpose you long for really is possible. Not because I have made it so but because God has made it so, and he is always faithful.

TUNING IN TO QUIET

When I was a kid, every radio had a large dial. To find the music station you wanted to listen to, you would turn the dial. When the radio wasn't tuned in to a specific station, you'd hear a loud static noise, but as you kept turning the dial, you'd eventually come across music. You would then slow the dial to find the perfect spot where the music came in the most clearly. This was called "tuning the radio." With this in mind, we will begin to "tune our hearts" to a much quieter "station"—a "sanctuary" if you will.

At the end of each chapter, you'll find a section called "Tuning in to Quiet," which will contain two parts. In "Contemplate," you'll find two or three reflection questions to consider. In "Cultivate," you'll learn about a practical way in which you can begin to tune your heart to a place of quiet solace. Lastly, but most importantly, you'll read a prayer that helps to bring each daily message home to your heart.

Contemplate

1. Do you feel unusually tired? Are you weary from online noise? Do you sense an inner restlessness, and you can't quite pinpoint the cause? Do you sometimes wish you could run away to a cabin in the woods or a remote island? If your answer is yes

to any of these questions, what do you think the source of your exhaustion might be? Write down whatever comes to mind.

2. How would you describe a quiet life to someone? What characteristics are common to people who are leading a quiet life?
3. What misconceptions might some people have about leading a quiet life?

Cultivate

Write down what you hope to gain throughout this 31-day journey. You can do this in a journal or a simple notebook, or you can download a free 31-Day Journal as a PDF at denisejhughes.com/31days. Even if you don't consider yourself an avid journal-keeper, begin to make it a regular practice to write a few words each day that capture your thoughts about your journey. The prompts on the free PDF will guide you!

Pray

Thank you, Lord, for consistently calling us to a quiet place with you: a place where the noise ceases and a new stillness in our souls can grow. Help us to recognize anew the many ways in which the world beckons us to conform to a pattern of ultra-performance and uber-productivity. Help us to find in you the sanctuary our hearts desperately need. We are so grateful for the peace you give. In your peace-filled name, Jesus, we pray. Amen.

Day 1

WHERE STRENGTH IS FOUND

"You will be delivered by returning and resting; your strength will lie in quiet confidence."

Isaiah 30:15

I went quiet.

I didn't announce my plan for a social-media sabbatical with a lengthy post on Instagram or Facebook, and I didn't preschedule any posts to go live during my absence. I just went quiet. I stopped posting, checking, and scrolling. I even deleted the social-media apps on my phone.

At first I noticed the way my right hand would instinctively reach for my phone. It surprised me how habitual the thumb-swiping had become, not to mention how mind-numbing the scrolling had been. It took a little while, but eventually my hand stopped reaching for my phone. In its place, I set some books and a Bible nearby. As I turned to other sources, and especially as I turned to *the* Source, I could feel my heart lighten. Freed from the tyranny of needing to see what everyone else was doing, I let quiet truth and beauty fill me.

During this process, I decided to do a study of the sanctuaries in the Bible. The first sanctuary, of course, was the Garden of Eden. It was a place of perfect tranquility, where the first humans could walk with God and chat about their day as casually as friends strolling through a park. But because of their eventual disobedience, they were cast out of this perfect sanctuary and barred from entering God's presence thereafter. And yet, God showed them mercy by promising that a path back into his presence was forthcoming.

A Tabernacle of Quiet

True to his word, God later instructed Moses saying, "Let them make me a sanctuary, that I may dwell in their midst" (Exodus 25:8). God even told Moses how to design this new sanctuary, for it was patterned after the sanctuary in heaven (Hebrews 8:5). This newly constructed tabernacle consisted of three sections: the outer courtyard, the Holy Place, and the Most Holy Place.

Upon entrance to this sanctuary, the priests would immediately experience a new kind of quiet as the heavy drapes of the tabernacle's walls kept out the noise of the world. This was even truer in that most inner place. Nineteenth-century English pastor Charles Spurgeon describes it, saying:

> *There was this peculiarity about [the Most Holy Place] . . . it was the shrine of unbroken quiet. Was ever a voice heard in it? Once in the year the high priest went in and filled it full of the smoke of incense as he waved his censer in the mystic presence, but otherwise it was a chamber in which there was no footfall of living thing, or voice of mortal man. Here was the home of absolute quiet and silence.*[1]

This was God's dwelling place—"the home of absolute quiet and silence." Back then, of course, only the high priest could enter that inner sanctum, and even then just once a year, but

There's something about stillness and a corresponding quietness of heart that is inviting, especially for those of us who live in a world full of hustle and never-ending noise.

the quietness of this sanctuary reflected the reality that in God's presence our hearts are quieted.

There's something about stillness and a corresponding quietness of heart that is inviting, especially for those of us who live in a world full of hustle and never-ending noise. We long for a place where the chaos of our daily lives is supplanted with a peace that cannot be described. We long for sanctuary, and we're hardly the first people to desire it.

Too often, though, we try to create our own "gardens" of paradise. This could be anything that gives us a reprieve, and this is especially true of our phones. They allow us to shed the physical limitations of our locale so we can enter digital realms. There, we can meet more people, have more conversations, and learn more things. We can even take on new identities. If we happen to feel disenfranchised from the actual community we live in, we can easily escape to an online realm and reinvent ourselves. It's all very exciting, but the answer isn't found in a paradise of our own making. Nor is the answer found in a paradise of someone else's making.

Where the Answer Is Found

These days a social-media sabbatical is nothing new. Taking a break or fasting from social media is a growing trend and for good reason. We are changed for the better when we look to truth more than YouTube. But if we could fix the tiredness in our souls or the disinterest in our hearts with periodic breaks from social media, then that's all we would need to do—schedule ourselves some routine breaks. But we can't fix ourselves. Life doesn't work that way.

The answer isn't simply in taking a break from social media, although it's not a bad idea for a lot of reasons. The real answer is in the words of the ancient prophet Isaiah, who said,

"You will be delivered by returning and resting; your strength will lie in quiet confidence" (Isaiah 30:15). By "returning," the prophet means repenting. When we repent from looking to earthly means to fill us and return to God as our sole life-sustaining source, we experience the genuine rest our hearts need.

Maybe you have struggled with the number of hours you spend each day on your phone. Or maybe social media hasn't had that much pull over you. Maybe your struggle is with something else. It will be different for each of us. But the starting point is the same for everyone. To experience a quiet heart that is truly at rest in Christ, we must first repent of looking to anything other than God to satisfy us. Finding  sanctuary begins with repentance: with acknowledging that we can't fix the malaise that plagues our souls. But God can, and our confidence rests in him alone.

TUNING IN TO QUIET

Contemplate

1. Have you ever taken an extended sabbatical from social media? If so, what was it like? What, if anything, did you learn or gain from that experience? If not, what has held you back?
2. What are some ways in which people today try to create their own "gardens" of paradise? In other words, what kinds of things seem to offer people a chance to shed their limitations and perhaps find an earthly sanctuary or temporary reprieve?

Cultivate

Is there an area in your life about which you feel a deep sense of dread or unease at the thought of giving it up? Write down any areas in your life that come to mind. Then consider whether or not these might be things or people you lean on more than God. If so, ask God for his forgiveness and bask in the knowledge that when "we confess our sins, he is faithful and righteous to forgive us our sins and to cleanse us from all unrighteousness" (1 John 1:9). In doing this, you are, in effect, "returning and resting," just as Isaiah prescribed, and inviting God to take it from there.

Pray

Lord, thank you for the gift of your grace so we can live in your presence forever. Forgive us when we are tempted to look to anything or anyone other than you to sustain us. Help us to keep our eyes fixed firmly on you, for peace begins and ends with you. We love you. In your precious name, Jesus, we pray. Amen.

Day 2

A NEW IDENTITY IN A NEW WORLD

"Therefore, if anyone is in Christ, he is a new creation; the old has passed away, and see, the new has come!"

2 Corinthians 5:17

Many of us recognize the way online noise depletes us, and we notice the difference it makes when we take extended social-media sabbaticals. But then, after a time, we usually return to the same fount of noise. I am no exception. Why is that? If a lengthy online pause leads to a freer and lighter heart, why do so many of us go back?

To explain this pattern, a computer scientist from Duke University, Chris Bail, offers a key insight. He says the source of our addiction to social media is not the comfort of our echo chambers or even the regular dopamine rush in our brains as conventional wisdom often explains it; rather, he says, social media is addictive precisely because "it makes it so much easier for us to do what is all too human: perform different identities, observe how other people react, and update our presentation of self to make us feel like we belong."[2] In other words, the reason why social media has become such a powerful mainstay in our lives is because it is where identity formation is now taking place.

The Formation of Online Identities

Where previous generations often sought to build their identities through work, those of today's generation seek to create an identity through an online persona. When kids today are asked what they want to be when they grow up, they no longer say a fireman or doctor or teacher. Instead, they want to be a YouTube star or an Instagram influencer.[3] Through the internet, people can create and recreate virtually limitless editions of their identities. This is now considered a common practice, which isn't a surprise given the strong emphasis in online circles to create a personal brand.

When I study the types of posts I see most often in my feed, several common brands stand out. Some of these online brands might be summed up as Bible Teacher Betty, Do-It-Yourself Deidra, Mom-Girlfriend Mandy, Homeschooler Holly, Transformation Trudy, Oily Olivia, Fitness Fiona, and so many more. I'm not poking fun, either. Believe me, I've been there.

There is nothing inherently wrong with creating an online brand, just as there is nothing wrong with generating some income through that brand. What I am wanting us to see, though, is how the internet has become something more than a place to find information, share ideas, and pass the time; it's become *the* place where we form our identities, and sometimes those identities become sources of income, which further cements the need to continue the online identity we have created. All of this means that when the noise of the online world becomes too much, there is a very real incentive—and sometimes a monetary incentive—to continue participating in the cycle of noise.

One of the things I came to realize was that the noise-makers are not just "out there" on the internet, but that I

In Scripture, we have an invitation to step into the sanctuary of God's presence, where we discover the truth about who we are and how we were made and what our purpose in life really is.

too was perpetuating some of the same noise in my own tiny corner of the web. To turn off the noise, I had to risk pressing the mute button on my online identity, and that's the dilemma facing so many of us today. If we simply go quiet online, what happens to our online identity?

Who We Really Are

In Scripture, we have an invitation to step into the sanctuary of God's presence, where we discover the truth about who we are and how we were made and what our purpose in life really is. In God's sanctuary, we not only find deep quiet and soul rest; we also find everything our identity-driven hearts have been longing for.

This is what Paul discovered, too. Before he ever penned those strangely paradoxical words instructing us to "seek to lead a quiet life," he experienced a massive identity shift. He started out as a devout person who followed all the rules of his religious world, and there were a lot of rules to follow! He conformed to his religious culture with such zeal that he led military campaigns to punish, and even execute, anyone who dared not to conform (Acts 8:1-3). It was an early form of cancel culture. And it formed Paul's entire identity.

Then Paul met Jesus and, through the power of the Holy Spirit, became a different person (9:1-19). He exchanged his sword for a pen and became a leading voice for a groundswell of others who were also following a new way to live. They called themselves the people of the Way (v 2). But first, Paul withdrew to the quiet of the desert, where he spent three years quietly relearning everything he thought he once knew (Galatians 1:11-24). Instead of looking to the religious structures of his day to form his identity, as he once had, Paul now looked to the Scriptures to know the one true God, and then, as a byproduct, he also came to understand himself more fully.

Paul's true identity was not formed by looking inside himself or by looking to the world around him; rather, his true identity took shape as he quietly looked to God in his word. The same can be said of us. When we look to the Maker of the universe, we also grow in our understanding of ourselves. In Christ we are new creations. So, we don't have to cling to a self-made identity online because God has already given us a new identity in himself.

We don't have to be Bible Teacher Betty or Fitness Fiona or Oily Olivia or any of the other online brands. Instead of an identity that is created by us, we find in the sanctuary our truest identity, which is conferred on us by God himself. So, when the noise and restlessness of this world wearies us to no end, we can confidently step away for a time, and perhaps even for an extended period of time, because we know where our true identity is found, and we know where true peace is found—in God's presence, in his holy sanctuary.

TUNING IN TO QUIET

Contemplate

1. What might you miss if you take some time off from social media or one of your favorite social apps?
2. Just as God gave Paul a new identity, God gives every person who believes in him a new identity (2 Corinthians 5:17). How has knowing Christ as your Savior changed you?

Cultivate

Consider your own online usage and ask yourself which online activities tend to give you a sense of identity. Then choose one online activity you enjoy and consider giving it up for the duration of these 31 days. It could be a social app, like Instagram or Voxer, or it could be an online game. It could be anything that serves as additional "noise" in your life. By giving this up, you will be creating space in your life for something else—something quieter and more fulfilling—which we will talk about in the next chapter.

Pray

> *Lord, thank you for the new life you have given us. Because of you, we can know who we really are. We are your daughters, and we don't need to drive ourselves to exhaustion, creating our own identities or brands. We can confidently step away from the noise of the world for a time because we know exactly who you say we are, and in this we can rest. In your sweet name, Jesus, we pray. Amen.*

Day 3

THE MIRRORS IN OUR HANDS

"We all, with unveiled faces, are looking as in a mirror at the glory of the Lord and are being transformed into the same image from glory to glory; this is from the Lord who is the Spirit."

2 Corinthians 3:18

"We need to go!" I texted my college-age daughter while I waited in the car. A few minutes later she climbed into the backseat with her makeup bag and phone. In my rearview mirror, I could see her applying makeup, except she wasn't holding a mirror in her hand. She was holding up her phone.

"Why are you holding your phone like that?" I asked.

"I'm using it as a mirror. This is how all my friends put on makeup."

Huh? I never thought of doing that. I guess it made sense, but it still seemed strange. I imagined teen girls everywhere, using the reverse camera lens on their phones to apply makeup. In more ways than one, our phones are like little mirrors, reflecting our image back to us. But our phones aren't the only mirrors in our lives.

The world loves to offer us a variety of manmade mirrors in an attempt to tell us who we are. Some of us may see our jobs as a reflection of our true selves, conflating what we do with who we are. Others of us may look to our spouses or our kids as a reflection of who we are. We see their accomplishments as our accomplishments, or their failures as our failures. Books on personality types are like a mirror, too. After taking a quick assessment, we turn to the section that tells us about our type. We gaze into the chapter, hoping to catch a reflection of who we really are. For me, a good report card at school was my mirror of choice. Maybe for you it was something else. We all have certain "mirrors" we look to, hoping to glean greater insight into who we are.

Like a house of mirrors, though, every manmade mirror communicates an image that impacts how we view ourselves and the world around us, and oftentimes these distorted self-images become internal noise, reverberating in our souls. This internal noise can sound like *"I wish I was prettier. I wish I was smarter. I wish I was more successful in my career. I wish I was less serious and more fun. I wish I was thinner. I wish I was more popular. I wish, I wish, I wish…"* This is what manmade mirrors do. Instead of showing us who we truly are, they can make us question and doubt ourselves, so that we wish we could be someone we're not.

But there is another house that is not a house of mirrors, but a house where there is such a sweet relief because the focus isn't on us but on Christ.

The House without Mirrors

Notably, that old tent-sanctuary had but one entrance. There were no side doors, for God's people were to understand that there is only one entrance into his presence.[4] But before the

We never find peace by focusing on ourselves. It's only when we stop focusing on ourselves that we find the door to freedom.

priests could enter, they had to wash their hands and feet in a large bronze laver, or what we might call a washbasin. The metal they used for the bronze laver came from the bronze mirrors the Hebrew women had given. Back then they didn't have glass mirrors like we do today. Instead, their mirrors were made from highly polished bronze that could reflect a person's image.

Moses writes, "He made the bronze basin and its stand from the bronze mirrors of the women who served at the entrance to the tent of meeting" (Exodus 38:8). Picture a group of women lining up to donate their bronze mirrors—probably one of their most prized possessions from the Egyptians. Their mirrors were then melted down to form a huge basin dedicated to cleansing. Where that bronze metal had once shown a reflection of themselves, it now presented them with a picture of the coming Christ, for he is the one who cleanses us and grants us entry into the sanctuary of God's presence.

I can't help but wonder if some of the women were sad to hand over their mirrors. Or did they give them gladly? Would we be as willing to hand over our mirrors? Maybe we wouldn't mind giving up some of our actual mirrors, but would we be ok with giving up those other "mirrors" that give us an earthly sense of who we are? In a discussion about these bronze mirrors, my friend Kate Battistelli wisely observes, "We will become what we behold, so let us behold Christ."[5] Yes, imagine that—a company of women reflecting Christ to the world. Imagine what could happen if we relinquished the mirrors of this world and sought to behold, instead, the truth and beauty of Christ through the one true mirror of the living word.

The One True Mirror

Worldly "mirrors" provide a limited view of ourselves at best and a distorted view of ourselves at worst. But the word of

God is also likened to a mirror, except that it is the only place where we will find a true reflection of who we really are (James 1:22-25). But we don't turn to Scripture to learn more about ourselves. First and foremost, we turn to Scripture to learn more about God in Christ, and as we gaze on him, we are transformed into his image. We become more like Jesus.

This is what we learn in the sanctuary of God's presence: we never find peace by focusing on ourselves. It's only when we stop focusing on ourselves that we find the door to freedom.

This isn't to say that it is somehow wrong for us to use a mirror for our normal get-ready routines. I think we're all glad to be able to check our teeth in a mirror for any remnants of this morning's breakfast. But we do want to become more cognizant of what we devote our gaze to, for we grow a quiet heart when we know where our true identity lies.

Friends, you are more than your job title. More than your achievements. More than your grade-point average. More than your marital status. More than your motherhood status. More than your bank account balance. More than your social-media influence. And more than your jeans size.

You are more than the worst thing you have ever done. And more than the best thing you have ever done. You are more than the worst thing that has ever been said about you. And more than the best thing that has ever been said about you.

You are more than the suffering you endure. And more than the circumstances around you. You are more than any label this world tries to put on you because you are not of this world; you are made for another world. An eternal world where there is no disease, no decay, and no despair. If you believe in the risen Jesus as Lord, you are a daughter of the King. This is who you really are. And it all begins in the sanctuary of his presence.

TUNING IN TO QUIET

Contemplate

1. If we become what we behold, what are you beholding on a daily or even hourly basis?
2. How do these things shape the way you view yourself?
3. How might gazing into God's word on a daily basis shape how you view God, the world, and yourself?

Cultivate

At the end of the previous chapter, you were challenged to consider giving up a source of noise or distraction in your life, such as a social-media app or some other online activity, especially one that gives you a sense of identity. Now let's fill that space by focusing our attention on the mirror of God's word. If reading the Bible hasn't been a daily part of your routine, try incorporating it into the natural rhythm of your day. If you're not sure where to start, begin by reading a few proverbs or a psalm each day. And if you are already in the habit of reading the Bible each day, go one step further and write out the verse at the top of each chapter in this book into your journal or notebook.

Pray

Thank you, Lord, that we don't need to look into any mirror in this world to discover who we are for we can look to you, the one who made us. Help us to look each day into the mirror of your word and to gaze upon your beauty. Because of you, we are freed from the pressure to reflect a certain image to those around us. You call us your daughter and that is enough because you are our Father, and in you we find rest. In your tender name, Jesus, we pray. Amen.

Day 4

HAVING A ONE-THING HEART

"I have asked one thing from the LORD*; it is what I desire: to dwell in the house of the* LORD *all the days of my life."*

Psalm 27:4

Sometimes I'm distracted by the multitude of messages coming at me on my phone. Other times I'm distracted by the circumstances around me. School. Work. Church. Friends. Family. Neighbors. You name it. There's always something that needs doing or someone who needs my attention. And there are days when it feels like too much. Like my heart is being stretched in a thousand different directions and I cannot possibly tackle one more thing. The temptation, then, is to check out for a little while with some mindless scrolling. Do you ever feel that way, too? Do you ever tire of the circumstances that pull you in different directions? Do you sometimes retreat from the many demands of everyday life with a little scrolling on your phone?

If you and I could sit together in a quiet corner of a quaint café, I'd want to lean in close and listen to you share from your heart, and when it was my turn, I'd probably confess that, every so often, I grow weary from all the demands and distractions. I want to exchange the worries that consume me for a quiet sense of peace.

The Prayer That Changes Everything

Thankfully, Scripture shows us that we're not alone when we feel overwhelmed by the cares of this world. In Psalm 27, the writer, David, knew all too well what it was like to live amid deeply troubling circumstances. In less than 14 verses, he mentions his enemies seven times (v 2, 6, 11, 12). He calls them his adversaries, foes, evildoers, and false witnesses. David is feeling completely assailed by his enemies. And yet, where does he place his confidence? What is the one thing he asks for?

In verse 4 he declares, "I have asked one thing from the LORD; it is what I desire: to dwell in the house of the LORD all the days of my life, gazing on the beauty of the LORD and seeking him in his temple." This is the prayer that changes everything. When it feels like life is being stretched too thin, David knows who holds every circumstance in his hands. He knows who orders the universe and orchestrates every good thing. David's confidence is in God, so his one request is that he will dwell in the house of the Lord all the days of his life.

I want that to be my prayer, too. I want to look to God first whenever life goes sideways. But sometimes I need to be reminded where—and to whom—to turn to.

David lived prior to the temple being built, so when he uses words like "temple" and "house of the Lord," he is referring to that ancient tent-sanctuary, the tabernacle, because that is where God dwelled. Today, we know God's Spirit dwells inside us as believers, and we can talk to him from anywhere. It's not like there's magical fairy dust inside a church building, but every church building does stand as a quiet reminder that there's a place where God's people gather. We are never alone.

A divided heart is at the root of all restlessness. The only solution is having a one-thing heart.

I wish I could say that I always desire to gaze on the Lord in his sanctuary when I'm experiencing a difficult season. Instead, my gaze is usually fixed on the reality facing me. My worries consume me, and my fears get the better of me. Maybe you've been there, too.

David's words are offered as a sweet reminder for each of us to lift our eyes, to retrain our focus, and to remember that no circumstance—neither yours nor mine—is ever beyond God's reach. And the one thing we can always be grateful for is that God is always in control. We can relinquish every care and concern into his capable hands.

When Our Worries Are Many

When our worries are many, it's likely because our hearts are divided by so many concerns, and a divided heart is at the root of all restlessness. The only solution is having a one-thing heart, but we can't produce one on our own. I know I've tried but, as the wise hymn-writer says, our hearts are prone to wander. And yet, this is my prayer: to trade my anxious heart for a heart that wants only one thing—to dwell in the house of the Lord; to gaze upon his beauty; and to inquire in his temple.

May this be your prayer, too. To have a one-thing heart. To have a heart that isn't distracted or divided but completely at rest in Christ. So, when the world's noise reaches deafening levels, you can remain steadfast and sure because God is steadfast and sure.

TUNING IN TO QUIET

Contemplate

1. How do our cares and worries add to the noise in our restless hearts?

2. How would you describe a quiet heart to someone? What does a quiet heart look like and feel like?

Cultivate

If a divided heart is at the root of all restlessness, then our aim is to have an undivided heart. But how? How can we stitch together the fragmented cares and worries of our hearts? We can begin by laying each care at God's feet. Today, enter the sanctuary of God's presence and list the ways in which you feel stretched right now. Invite God into each of those circumstances. Ask for his wisdom. Then ask God to give you a one-thing heart—a heart that truly wants only one thing: Christ. Since the old sanctuary in the Bible pointed to Christ, we find sanctuary when we find rest in Christ's presence.

Pray

Lord, we don't want our hearts divided by worries. We don't want our minds preoccupied with fears. We want you. We really do. But far too often we falter in our wanting, so we are asking you to take up residence in those hidden places in our hearts where we are prone to be divided by our many wants and worries. Help us, Lord, to have an undivided heart. Help us, by your grace, to have a one-thing kind of heart, where the one thing we truly desire is to dwell in your presence forever. In your holy name, Jesus, we pray. Amen.

Day 5

A PLACE OF REFUGE

"The L*ORD ... is my refuge and my fortress, my God in whom I trust."*

Psalm 91:2

All this talk about entering the sanctuary might sound nice, and maybe a little poetic, but for some, the invitation to step into any kind of sanctuary might sound terrifying. The thought of walking inside the doors of a church might remind us of a stuffy Sunday morning service with a loud preacher who stood behind a large pulpit and yelled a lot. Or worse, it could dredge up painful memories of abuse at the hands of a clergyman.

Tragically, far too many souls have not been given the benefit of associating a sanctuary with a place of honesty and integrity, peace and well-being. In this broken world, too many sanctuaries have been anything but the sanctuary they were supposed to be.

If this has been your experience, I am so sorry. I understand how utterly disorienting it is when the person we once looked up to turns out to be someone totally different. When I was 14, my pastor—the one who baptized me in a river—left his family and left town. He then embraced a lifestyle that was completely counter to what he had once preached. A destroyed family and church parish were left in his wake. That pastor was also my father.

Reconciling Reality with Theology

I understand the deep disappointments and disillusionments that come when the very people we should be able to turn to are not the people we thought they were. When this happens, it spurs in us untold questions. Who can we turn to? Where can we go with our hurts and our questions? How can we trust anyone in a position of spiritual authority when we have personally experienced the heartbreak that comes when that authority has been abused? How can any sanctuary be deemed physically, emotionally, and spiritually safe?

Perhaps, in the secret chambers of your heart, you have asked some of these same questions. It's understandable. I have wrestled plenty with trying to reconcile my reality with my theology. But when I met Jesus, I was struck by how different he was, and I wanted to learn more about him. As I read page after page in the Bible, his love became so real, and the more I learned about Jesus, the more I knew I could trust him.

I want that for you, too. If you've ever felt shattered by an experience at church. If you've ever been betrayed by the people you thought were your spiritual advisors. If you've ever wondered if any sanctuary could ever be a place of safety. My prayer for you is that you will experience deep spiritual healing—the kind that only comes from spending time with Jesus. Because he will never disappoint. When we put our faith in God and not in humans, we are never disappointed because he alone is trustworthy and sure.

A quiet life is
characterized by a
quiet confidence
that God is good.

So, if the thought of stepping into what is sometimes referred to as a sanctuary—a church building—is the last thing you want to do right now, I understand, but if you continue this journey into a real sanctuary—the one found in the quiet pages of Scripture—together we can grow in our understanding of who God is: the real God. The one who knew you before you were born and called you by name. The one who sees in you what no one else sees and wants for you what no one else can fathom. This is the God we can put our faith in. This is the God we can trust.

The Journey Forward

In Psalm 91, when the psalmist asserts that God is his refuge and the one in whom we can place our trust, he is speaking from experience. And the same can be said of us. When we walk with God, we experience his provision and protection in countless ways. God's consistency in this manner creates in us a deep, abiding assurance that God is, in fact, our safe refuge: someone we can always turn to.

Warren Wiersbe, a beloved old pastor—who remained faithful to God and his family through his final days—once said this about Psalm 91:1-2: "The most important part of a believer's life is the part that only God sees, the 'hidden life' of communion and worship that is symbolized by the Holy of Holies in the Jewish sanctuary." Today, we no longer have priests entering the sanctuary on our behalf. Instead, we are invited directly into God's presence, and when we spend time with God in the sanctuary of his presence, we grow in trust and confidence and assurance.

A quiet life is characterized by a quiet confidence that God is good. He is good when others let us down, and he is good when our circumstances are not. He is good in his love for us, and he is good in his intentions toward us. When we have this settled in our hearts, so much of the internal noise we carry fades away.

Maybe your story has never known the heartache of a so-called sanctuary that was anything but. If so, then give God thanks and ask him how you can be an instrument of peace for others. But if your story has known the heartbreaking reality of this terribly broken world, it's ok to tell God about your hesitancy to step inside another sanctuary. Ask him to reveal more of himself to you as you explore his sanctuary in Scripture. Invite him to penetrate the darkness of those painful memories with his light. Ask him to make a way for there to be hope again because bringing light into darkness happens to be his specialty.

TUNING IN TO QUIET

Contemplate

1. Name some of the safest places you have ever known. What did those places have in common?
2. Whenever I think of the safest places I have known, they weren't just locations; they included special people who were always safe to be around. Who have those safe people been in your life?
3. How is Jesus different from every other person you have ever met? What are some of his attributes?

Cultivate

Old wounds have a way of walling us off from others. Believe me, I know. So, before we venture much further in this 31-day journey, prayerfully consider who you might ask to join you along the way—someone you can trust, someone who is for you, and, above of all, someone who is wholeheartedly committed to serving Christ. Perhaps you can share your story with this trusted friend. Healing rarely happens in isolation. That's why it's so important to have someone you trust walking alongside you. Then in your journal make a list of all the reasons why you can always—ALWAYS!—trust Jesus.

Pray

Lord, thank you that you are good and you are trustworthy. When people let us down and life doesn't turn out as we thought it would, help us to turn to you. Reveal yourself to us more and more so that our eyes always see you. Heal those places inside us where deep wounds have taken hold, and help us to know—to truly know—that you are our good Father, and in your hands we are held for you are our refuge. In your trustworthy name, Jesus, we pray. Amen.

Day 6

WHEN LIGHT PIERCES DARKNESS

"This is the message we have heard from him [Jesus] and declare to you: God is light, and there is absolutely no darkness in him."

1 John 1:5

Sometimes we're reluctant to find solace in a sanctuary because there's just too much sadness lingering in our souls. Life has been hard, and hope has been harder to come by. But sadness is never stagnant. When left unattended too long, it has a way of turning into despair. This despair then casts a shadow over everything. The only antidote to such darkness in the soul is light.

When the year has been longer and darker than anyone could have imagined, we need light. When the unspoken losses have painted the year with a darkness that's palpable, we need light. When the dreams we once held have been crushed by unforeseen suffering, we need light. When the isolation and loneliness have pressed in so deep that it's hard to breathe, we need light. And when the people we love most have been taken from us, we fiercely and desperately need light.

Maybe your year has been marked by sadness. Or maybe you're in a good place. Whatever season you may find yourself in at the moment, it's always good to remember that it was into the darkness that God came. With his very presence he dispelled all shadows. And that sanctuary of old, the tabernacle, presented the perfect picture of this truth.

The Single Source of Light

At the entrance to the tabernacle that Moses and the Israelites constructed, we would have seen the large bronze basin where the priests washed their hands and feet. Then as we moved from the outer courtyard into the Holy Place, we would notice two things. First, we would notice the immediate sense of quiet. Second, we would notice that there were no windows or skylights.

The only light by which we could see would have come from the gold lampstand with seven lamps. If you picture in your mind a menorah, with three branches on each side of the candlestick's center, you'll have a close idea of what the gold lampstand looked like inside the Holy Place (Exodus 25:31-40). It was made from one talent of pure gold, which was the equivalent of 75 pounds (34kg), and it was elaborately engraved with almond blossoms.[6] The light didn't come from wax candles, either, but from the oil that people gave. Thus, the only light inside the sanctuary came from this one source. This is significant because it represented the one true Light of the world. Where there would otherwise be total darkness, God is the only true source of light.

Like the bronze basin outside the entrance, the gold lampstand inside the Holy Place pointed to Christ, the Light of the world. Indeed, every aspect of this sanctuary foreshadowed the coming Christ. So, the better we understand the components that made up the sanctuary, the better we will understand the fullness of Jesus. *

Christianity is not a religion of dos and don'ts. It's the story of Light coming to drive out the darkness.

In our day and age, we look back to the birth of Christ, but for Moses and the Israelites, they could only look forward with great hope. The sanctuary, then, gave them a more concrete picture, and one of those pictures was the coming Light, who would penetrate the darkness.

The Story of Light

The other day I saw a meme that proudly stated, "Having a religion is fine, as long as you don't tell other people how to live." The maker and sharer of this meme reduced religion to a rulebook—a list of dos and don'ts. Which is sad because that's not what Christianity is about. It's not a religion of dos and don'ts. It's the story of Light coming to drive out the darkness.

Consider the theme of light that has pulsed throughout all of history. In the beginning, there was a vast darkness. Then God said, "Let there be light," and there was light (Genesis 1:1-5). Just like that. His spoken word separated the light from the darkness, and God has continued to separate light from darkness ever since. When the first man and woman rebelled, darkness entered their hearts, and that darkness has been passed on to every generation since. But God made a promise that one day an eternal Light would enter the world, and this Light would overcome darkness, once and for all (John 1:1-5).

As the years passed, believers in the promise looked for the Light. Then one night, a new star lit up the blackened sky, pointing to the promise born. Wealthy men traveled from the east while poor shepherds came in from the fields. Rich and poor alike, they came to see the promised Light—a tiny baby, entrusted to a teenage girl and a simple man (Matthew 1:18-25; 2:1-12; Luke 2:8-16).

It's no coincidence that Jesus was born in the dark of night with a new star shining brightly overhead. The Light of the world had come. Today, we celebrate Christmas with the gift of hindsight, and obviously, the world has done its best to mix a lot of loud commercialism into what was originally the Christian celebration of the birth of Christ. Christmas nowadays can be one of the noisiest times of the year with all the jingling bells and ho-ho-hos. But even then, we still see lights hanging everywhere. Every light is a reminder that God did not leave us to fend for ourselves in a world given to darkness (John 3:19). The Light has come. Christianity is the story of the Light, who came and dispelled the darkness that tried to overtake us.

I know how dark the world is because there was a season when sadness overwhelmed me. And it was there, in the midst of suffocating darkness, where the story of Light shone the brightest. When I couldn't find light or joy or hope in anything, I turned to Jesus, and he didn't shame me for feeling low. He didn't berate me for not exhibiting more gratitude. He remembered that I am but dust. And he reminded me that he is in control. He didn't change my circumstances, but he did show me that if I trust him, in the end everything will turn out all right. It may not happen in the timeframe I'd prefer, but again, time belongs to him. And he gave me reason to hope again.

This is my story. It can be anyone's story, too. While the broken parts of our stories are painfully real, Christ's redemption restores us and re-stories us.

I may not know your story, but I can tell you that Jesus is a real person. You can tell him all about the darkness you're dealing with, and you can ask him to drive it away. He'll do it, too. It's what he loves to do. I'm not saying he'll make your life all rosy and cheery. But he will fill you with his light, and a newfound hope will be yours forever. And no power in hell can ever take it away from you.

That's what we find in the sanctuary. We find the God of light.

TUNING IN TO QUIET

Contemplate

1. Have you ever known a season of sadness, when it felt as if the darkness was closing in? How has the God of light already spoken hope into those times and seasons?
2. Articulate in your own words how the single source of light in that old tent-sanctuary points us to Christ.

Cultivate

Today, let's do something super easy but always life-giving. In the evening, slip outside to catch those final moments when that ring of fire in the heavens drops from view. I like to think of every sunset as a promise, knowing that light will come again soon. (And if you're reading this after the sun has already gone down, set your alarm to wake up early and watch the sun rise!) One of the simplest ways in which we can cultivate a quiet life is by intentionally pausing each day to watch the light God hung in the sky while giving praise that he is the Light of the world.

Pray

Lord, thank you that we are never left to fend off the sadness in our souls on our own. But as we enter your presence, your light dispels every shadow. For you are the Light of the world, and in you there is no darkness at all. We thank you for the light you bring into our hearts, and we ask that you help us share your light with others. For this is your story. In your light-filled name, Jesus, we pray. Amen.

Day 7

THE GRACE OF GOOD WORK

"For the LORD your God has blessed you in all the work of your hands. He has watched over your journey through this immense wilderness. The LORD your God has been with you these past forty years, and you have lacked nothing."

Deuteronomy 2:7

I didn't wake up one day and decide to give the quiet life a try. My journey toward cultivating a different way to live was birthed in a season when my life was anything but quiet. I had all the signs of being a workaholic:

- I buried myself in my work.
- I took on more projects than was reasonably expected.
- I neglected my health and never exercised.
- I regularly chose work over sleep.
- My stress levels were constantly elevated. (Hello, cortisol.)
- I was all work and no play; seriousness pervaded my mood every day.
- I didn't have time to go on a vacation, and if I did go, I took work with me.

- And here's the real kicker: I liked it. In fact, I loved it.

I like working. I find deep satisfaction in a job well done, and I look forward to the next project. But my work pace was taking a toll not only on my health but on my relationships as well. Something needed to change, so I did what I do best: I conducted research. I launched myself into a personal study on the theology of work.

How does God feel about work? What does the Bible say about work? Are there limits to how much a person should work? If work is a good thing, and I believe it is, how do we as humans turn it into an unhealthy thing? Why does work become all-consuming for some and not others? How can we create healthier work lives not only for ourselves but also for the sake of our loved ones?

These questions spurred me on through countless books and articles on the topic, and it became painfully obvious that I am not alone. Overworking has become a way of life in North American culture. In our individualistic society, work is upheld as a guaranteed path to self-actualization, by which you become the best version of yourself. But overworking is the opposite of living with a quiet heart. It requires an intensity and drive that is unsustainable in the long run, and it stems from an inner restlessness.

While I enjoyed my work, my level of enjoyment was dissipating as my health concerns were rising. In many respects, I was "living my dream," but somewhere along the way, my work had become all-consuming, and the cost proved too steep. The subtle effects of conformity—to a loud culture that promotes work as the path to personal fulfillment—had crept into my life to the detriment of my well-being. To my

When I remember that God is the true provider, I can relinquish my tendency to overwork, and I can embrace the God-ordained rhythms of rest.

own surprise, I had withdrawn from real life while working like mad behind my computer to finish each project.

Work can be many things to different people. For some, work can be a source of identity. For others, work is a means of accumulating more stuff. A bigger house. A nicer car. A fancier vacation. For me, I think my inclination to overwork revealed a hidden lack of trust. Somewhere deep inside, I felt that I needed to work just in case God didn't come through. I know that sounds silly, but it's true. I needed the manna reminder.

The Manna Reminder

Inside that old tabernacle-sanctuary, the Most Holy Place held one thing—the ark of the covenant—which represented the presence of God. The ark contained three articles: the stone tablets with the Ten Commandments, Aaron's staff, and a golden urn that held the manna (Hebrews 9:4). The manna was bread from heaven that rained down every morning for the Israelites as they wandered in the wilderness. God literally provided food for his people each day; they never had to toil ceaselessly to acquire what they needed. And if they tried to hoard the manna, it would deteriorate, for they were to look to God each day as their provider. The manna inside the ark of the covenant, in the innermost part of the sanctuary, was a steady reminder of God's faithfulness to provide.

When I remember that God is the true provider, I can relinquish my tendency to overwork, and I can embrace the God-ordained rhythms of rest because I know that provision ultimately isn't up to me. Then I am free to enjoy my work for the gift of grace that it is.

To break the cultural conformity that had seeped into my work life, I asked God for forgiveness for trying to work my way into self-sufficiency. Then I started making changes, and many of those changes involved limits. I placed limits on how often each day I checked my work email, as well as the group Voxer account and the dozens of Slack channels. I radically limited the amount of caffeine I consumed each day as well. This allowed me to limit how late I could stay up working, and I began going to bed at a decent hour. Such limits may not be prescribed in Scripture, per se, but everything in the Bible points to God alone as being truly limitless; whereas we are finite creatures with certain God-designed limits. And when we live within our human limits, we are healthier for it.

Above all, I made the Sabbath a priority again, which is definitely prescribed in Scripture. When we limit our work to six days a week and receive the seventh day for rest, we honor God as the ultimate provider. (We'll talk about this a bit more in the next chapter, too.)

My work associates probably thought I was turning into some crazy Luddite when I was no longer available 24/7, but my family was enjoying having me around more, and I was beginning to feel like myself again. In the process, my ambitions changed, too. The things that had been important to me in my thirties were no longer a driving force in my forties. My goals changed.

Maybe you have experienced this inner restlessness, too, driving you to overwork. Or maybe an inner restlessness propels you into overdrive in other ways—overshopping, overeating, overexercising, or even over-watching a favorite TV show. A disordered heart drives us to take good things and distort them into ultimate things. A quiet heart is the antidote to overdoing it in any area of our lives, which is why it's necessary to make an honest examination of our heart's ambitions, which is what we'll do in the next chapter.

When Paul instructed the saints in Thessalonica to lead a quiet life, he had us in mind as well. It's not wrong to have ambition or work hard, but we want to remember who the real provider and sustainer is. The same one who provided the manna will provide for us as well.

TUNING IN TO QUIET

Contemplate

1. In what areas of your life do you have a tendency to overdo it? How might this tendency reveal a hidden lack of trust in God?
2. What kinds of limits might be helpful in those areas where you struggle? What are some practical ways in which you could begin to implement these limits?
3. How might an inner restlessness begin to turn into an inner quietness as a result of incorporating these healthier limits?

Cultivate

Maybe you already do this, but one of the simplest ways in which we can cultivate a quiet life is by setting for ourselves a consistent bedtime and sticking to it. This may seem silly or even juvenile. But our hearts experience a deep sense of settledness when we can reach the end of the day and say, "Thank you, Lord, for this day. I now leave the rest of the work waiting for me until tomorrow, for I know that I am not the real provider here; you are." Then let sleep come in the sweetest of ways.

Pray

Lord, you are the manna-maker and perfect provider. Forgive us when we think we can work to provide for ourselves in our own strength. Help us to remember that even the ability to work is a gift from you. Thank you for the grace of good work. May we be good stewards of the work you give us, and may we bring you glory in all we do. In your gracious name, Jesus, we pray. Amen.

Day 8

A TIMELY HEART X-RAY

"Search me, God, and know my heart; test me and know my concerns. See if there is any offensive way in me; lead me in the everlasting way."

Psalm 139:23-24

One day, while passing the food processors in Bed Bath & Beyond, I came across a large piece of wall art that said, "Dream until your dreams come true." I stopped mid-aisle and stared at those words. We encounter some version of this message everywhere we go: "Never give up on your dreams!" Indeed, one of the loudest messages in the Western world is for us to dream big and do all we can to pursue our dreams.

And yet, if we're "to seek to lead a quiet life," as Paul instructs in 1 Thessalonians 4:11, is this antithetical to dreaming big and pursuing our dreams? What does Paul mean when he says "to seek"?

In the original Greek, Paul uses the word *philotimeisthai*, which means "to strive earnestly" or "to pursue with zealous ambition."[7] This same passage in 1 Thessalonians 4:11 is sometimes translated as "Make it your *ambition* to lead a quiet life" (emphasis mine, NIV). So, is Paul saying we need to cast aside all of our personal dreams and earthly ambitions?

Is all ambition bad?

The answer is no. Not all dreams and ambitions are bad. There are two kinds of ambition, unholy ambition and holy ambition, and the Bible recognizes both kinds. In James 3:14 we're warned, "But if you have bitter envy and selfish ambition in your heart, don't boast and deny the truth." Here, ambition is described as selfish, but in Romans 15:20, Paul describes a different kind of ambition, saying, "It has always been my ambition to preach the gospel where Christ was not known" (NIV). Here, we see ambition is good when our desires are aligned with good ends and include good means.

Perhaps you've followed the world's advice to dream big, and the pursuit cost more than you bargained for. Perhaps you've chased a dream only to discover it was a mirage all along; the thing you pursued didn't even exist in the end. Or, perhaps you've run hard after a dream and achieved everything you once hoped for, but it didn't fulfill you like you thought it would.

How can you know if your ambitions are good and righteous? How can you be sure your ambitions are compatible with leading a quiet life?

Five Ways to Discern Holy Ambitions

In *Teach Us to Want: Longing, Ambition, and the Life of Faith*, Jen Pollock Michel asks, "How do we ever know when desire isn't the apple of self-actualizing promise leading us far from God? Can it be possible to trust our own hearts?"[8] This is a good question. Before we can make it our ambition to lead a quiet life, we must take an inventory of the ambitions that already have a firm place in our lives.

The following five questions will help us tease out any unholy ambitions lurking inside our hearts, but do keep in mind that these five questions are meant to be diagnostic, not condemnatory. Having holy ambitions isn't something we acquire once and for all; rather it's an ongoing process that requires the occasional heart check-up. So, let's take a heart x-ray of our ambitions.

1. Do you have relationships with people who cannot benefit you in any way?

In other words, do you regularly enjoy someone's company for the sheer sake of enjoying their company and not because your association with them could potentially benefit you in some way? Our response to this question reflects the ambition-direction of our hearts. When our ambitions are rightly aligned with God's word and directed toward good ends, we can enjoy the presence of individuals who may not have anything to offer in terms of a potential promotion or positive association. Unholy ambitions lead us to see people as resources and opportunities, whereas holy ambitions lead us to appreciate every person we encounter regardless of their station in life.

2. Do your ambitions or dreams take you away from your family to an inordinate degree?

Most of us can think of a season (or two) when we were incredibly busy—busy to the point where we weren't spending time with our families like we wanted to. But when a busy season turns into regular daily life, this is an indicator of an unholy ambition in our hearts. When our families continue to make sacrifices for our ambitions—with no end in sight—then it's time to reconsider our ambitions.

3. How committed are you to honoring and observing the Sabbath?

Observance of a God-ordained weekly Sabbath is a key litmus test. If we can't accomplish everything on our plates in six days and then rest on the seventh day, something is amiss. If we consistently feel that we must work seven days a week in order to get everything done, then our ambitions have veered into unholy territory. A Sabbath doesn't have to take place on a Sunday, either. Many folks have to work on Sundays, including pastors! Designating one day a week for rest is not only an act of living in obedience to Scripture; it is also paramount for our health, including the health of our souls, where idols of ambition can take root.

4. Are your ambitions or dreams about making God's name great or yours?

This can be tricky because oftentimes our dreams and ambitions are mixed with both good and not-so-good intentions. Part of us genuinely wants to see God's kingdom expanded, but in the process, we wouldn't mind being known as one of God's favorite agents in bringing about said expanded kingdom.

The same is true in a non-church context. Part of us sincerely wishes to see our work bring good outcomes for others, but in the process, we wouldn't mind being known as the person who helped bring about those good outcomes. It all comes down to credit. Are we ok if no one but God knows about our good deeds? If we can answer this question affirmatively, then our ambitions are likely in check.

5. Will you be ok with God if your ambitions or dreams never come about in this lifetime?

Let's say our ambitions and dreams have good ends and include good means. Let's say we're even ok with no one but God knowing about the good deeds we accomplish. But what if our dreams never come to fruition? If our biggest dreams and deepest longings are never realized, will we still follow after God? If our answer is yes, then that's a good indicator that our hearts' ambitions are on the right path.

Undressing Our Hearts

Writer Jen Pollock Michel says, "When we talk about desire, we undress our hearts."[9] These five questions help us "undress our hearts" by examining our true intentions. They serve as realignment checkpoints to help us disentangle the layers of our heart's desires. It's not always comfortable, but it's crucial if we're to lead a quiet life.

If you're anything like me, you've got a mix of both holy and unholy ambitions taking up residency in your heart. It's what it means to be human. And yet, this is something we can acknowledge in ourselves with honesty while also asking God to work on our hearts in these areas. God always welcomes our humble admissions and sincere pleas for his forgiveness, wisdom, and strength because keeping our ambitions in check is a necessary part of cultivating a quiet heart.

TUNING IN TO QUIET

Contemplate

1. What are the ambitions of your heart? (It's okay to be really honest here!)

2. Of the five diagnostic questions in this chapter, which one struck you as most poignant? Why do you think that is?
3. If others were to look at your life, would they say that leading a quiet life is one of your ambitions?

Cultivate

Sorting out our holy ambitions from our unholy ones is hard heart work, but it's so important. Our hearts are always restless when we are focused on ourselves and our less-than-holy ambitions. This is why a big part of cultivating a quiet life is leading an others-centered life. So, in returning to the first diagnostic question, can you think of someone in your life whom you can befriend for the sheer sake of enjoying that person's company and not for any other kind of benefit, either personally or professionally? Perhaps someone will come to mind right away. Or perhaps you'll want to pray awhile and ask God to bring someone to mind. Write down one specific way in which you can reach out to this person and then do it. Reach out. Make a connection. Give some of your time away. You may be surprised at what a blessing this relationship could be.

Pray

Lord, thank you that we can come to you for an honest heart x-ray, and no matter what we find, you offer us grace and forgiveness. As we seek to cultivate a quiet heart for quiet living, help us to ferret out any unholy ambitions lurking inside our hearts. Stir in us a different kind of ambition—an ambition to lead a quiet life. We ask this in Jesus' holy name. Amen.

Day 9

TO BE SEEN AND UNDERSTOOD

"Humble yourselves, therefore, under the mighty hand of God, so that he may exalt you at the proper time, casting all your cares on him, because he cares about you."

1 Peter 5:6-7

In the midst of a trying season, I found myself struggling in just about every way. Physically, I was battling a weird ailment that made me extremely uncomfortable, and for several weeks I had gotten less than four hours of sleep each night. Emotionally, I felt drained, like a lot was expected of me but very little refilled me. Spiritually, I was running on empty.

When I reached my lowest point, my exasperation got the better of me, and I did the very thing I always say not to do: I vented—in a group text no less. Sure, I'd had a rough go of it lately, but still, I never use digital means to let out my feelings, especially when I happen to be feeling down. I know it's better to share those things in person and in the context of a trusted relationship. I know better! But in one moment on one particularly hard day, I expressed some of my frustration to six colleagues in a group chat. I simply wanted someone to understand what I was going through. I wanted someone to see me.

Perhaps you've been there, too. Maybe you're there now. Maybe there's something happening in your personal life that nobody really knows about, and it's affecting your ability to function. Maybe you're dealing with a chronic health issue that impairs the way you relate to others. Maybe you're hurting over a fractured relationship. Maybe you've just gone through a major life change, and you're struggling to keep up. In those moments, we need a friend who can turn to us and say, "Whoa. You're juggling a lot right now. I can see you're carrying a heavy load."

When we're hurting, it helps to have someone who can see what we're going through and affirm that it really is hard. We're not imagining things, and we're not exaggerating. What we're going through is real, and we need to hear someone say it. Maybe that's why I broke my own rule about never venting digitally. I was miserable, and I wanted someone to see my misery. Typing out those words makes me laugh at the thought, but in that moment on that day, that's where I was at.

Where to Cast Our Cares

Thankfully, I know I'm not alone in my faltering. When we read the Bible, we step into the lives of real people who experienced real circumstances. Through Scripture, we follow the ups and downs of humans who oftentimes failed to live up to God's best for them. One of the most well-known examples of such outward failure is Peter. His passionate, yet impulsive nature sometimes got the better of him as he blurted out words he would immediately regret (Luke 22:54-62). Jesus, of course, would forgive Peter, and we see him grow through the years as he continued to follow Christ.

It's notable, then, that it's Peter who pens these words: "Humble yourselves, therefore, under the mighty hand

To lead a quiet life means knowing where to take our hurts and cares and concerns.

of God, so that he may exalt you at the proper time, casting all your cares on him, because he cares about you" (1 Peter 5:6-7). To humble yourself implies humbly accepting the circumstances to which one may be bound. This is, of course, easier said than done, but it also conveys a sense of trust in God's sovereignty over all things, knowing that one day he will, indeed, "exalt you at the proper time." In the meantime, we are called to cast our cares and anxieties on him (v 7). Not on the world at large. But on him.

That day when I broke my own rule and vented in a group text was a textbook case of not humbling myself "under the mighty hand of God." Instead, I chose to bring my cares to the digital feet of my colleagues.

Obviously, I haven't reached some state of tranquil perfection in this business about leading a quiet life. I'm a sinner who still needs God's grace on a daily basis. I have days when I get frustrated over big and little things alike, and I still have moments when I'm not at my best. But when those moments come, I know where I can go to find true rest.

We live in a world, though, where it's never been easier to find a sympathetic "friend" or a listening ear. With the tap of a screen, we can quickly find an audience of hundreds, if not thousands, of willing ears. The world beckons us to follow the new norm: Having a rough day? Share about it on Instagram. Experiencing a difficult season? Post about it on Facebook. Then sit back and watch as the heart-hugging emojis pop up on our screens to tell us that we're seen. This is our brave new world.

While everything from the mundane to the momentous fills our media feeds, the online noise that tends to garner the most attention is the kind that paints our pain in pixelated pictures. With memes and selfies, we tell the world how we're hurting, and the world responds. This helps us to know we're not alone. People are out there who get us and who care. We feel seen, and this is no small matter. As social-media users, however, our simple act of scrolling leads us to an abundance of strolling through other people's personal lives and vice versa. It's gotten to the point where very little is actually considered as "personal" anymore. Everything is potential fodder for the feed. And the level of noise continues to rise.

Perhaps it's unfair to characterize this type of sharing as "online noise." Some might argue that this is simply a way for people to communicate authentically what they're going through. But when I return to 1 Thessalonians 4:11, Paul clearly instructs Christ-followers "to seek to lead a quiet life, [and] to mind your own business." In other words, leading a quiet life happens *in conjunction* with minding our own business.

For a long time, I read that part about minding our own business as a command not to gossip, which is partly what Paul is saying. We shouldn't be so interested in the juicy affairs of others, but at the same time, Paul could also be implying that when we mind our own affairs, we are less inclined to lay our affairs at the world's feet.

Social media, of course, didn't exist in Paul's day, but the human heart is the same in every location and every time period. As humans, we regularly face the temptation to involve ourselves in other people's affairs and to involve others in ours. Paul's instructions, however, are counter to this basic human temptation. To lead a quiet life is to refrain from participating in gossip about others, and also to refrain from inviting others into our business. To lead a quiet life means knowing where to take our hurts and cares and concerns.

So, if you have ever blurted out something you immediately regretted, or pressed the "send" button and wished you could take it back, I understand. I've been there. Peter has too. Thankfully, we serve a God who forgives us when we repent and gives us a new start. He alone is the one who truly sees us, and he has created a place much healthier than social media where we can cast our cares (Hint: It's in the sanctuary), which is what we'll talk about in the next chapter.

TUNING IN TO QUIET

Contemplate

1. Have you ever shared something in a context where you later regretted sharing it? If you could do it all over again, what would you do differently?
2. How does social media encourage and legitimize sharing and even oversharing? How does this lend itself to more online noise?
3. God promises to exalt his followers "at the proper time," which could happen later in this life or in the next. How might this biblical truth encourage you as you experience, and sometimes endure, difficult circumstances in the here and now?

Cultivate

In our current digital climate, the temptation to speak impulsively or overshare in a public setting is always before us because that comes with certain rewards: namely, when we overshare, it brings a level of attention to our pain, and sometimes that helps, if even for a little while. But if we are serious about cultivating a quiet heart, we want to bring our cares to those who truly know us in a real-life context, which we will consider in more depth in the next chapter. Today, consider some ways in which you can follow Paul's command when he says we should mind our own business. Name one concern you've had lately, and instead of bringing it to others via a digital pathway, bring your concern directly to God by writing it out in your journal.

Pray

Lord, thank you for seeing us. In every situation, in every circumstance, you are there, and you see everything we are going through. You understand better than anyone, and we are never alone because you are with us. Forgive us when we are tempted to look in the wrong places for consolation. Help us to bring our cares to you above all else, for you alone can provide the comfort we need. In your comforting name, Jesus, we pray. Amen.

Day 10

THE ENCOURAGEMENT WE REALLY NEED

"When I am filled with cares, your comfort brings me joy."

Psalm 94:19

One time my family went tent-camping and my daughter's inflatable mattress kept deflating. It wouldn't happen right away, but almost imperceptibly, over the course of a couple of hours, the air in her mattress would slowly leak out until the mattress was flat again. We looked and looked for a tiny pinprick of a hole, and we tried to listen for the faintest whisper of escaping air. But we couldn't find the hole to patch it.

The same is true with a lot of the "encouragement" we find on social media. It may "fill us" for a few minutes or a few hours, but eventually, that kind of temporary encouragement ebbs away, leaving us feeling emptier than before and looking for another quick fill-up.

For instance, it's standard fare for some social-media influencers to tell us, "If you are hurting right now, I want you to know I see you." In those moments, such words might feel comforting, but it's a fleeting comfort because when someone we've never met types those words onto a screen from a thousand miles away, they can't really see us. They can't really know our situation. They might be able to make good guesses, and they might be able to convey some general truths, but the comfort they provide is short-lived.

Bringing Together a Community

The more I study Scripture, the more I'm convinced that God has already created an appropriate setting where humans can share and commune with him and others, especially when going through difficult times. We were never meant to suffer in solitude, but neither were we meant to make our business everybody's business. There's a healthier way to share and to commune with God and others, and it's in his sanctuary.

In the Old Testament God gathered a large extended family that worked as slaves in Egypt before he brought them to a place where they could be free. He did it in dramatic fashion, too. He parted the Red Sea and led his people to freedom by a pillar of cloud by day and a pillar of fire by night. It's the stuff of lore, only real. And there, in the middle of a wilderness, God gave them instructions to build a sanctuary.

After God's people followed his instructions, the glory of the Lord filled the tabernacle, and the final verse in Exodus says, "For the cloud of the LORD was over the tabernacle by day, and there was a fire inside the cloud by night, visible to the entire house of Israel throughout all the stages of their journey" (40:38). This newly built sanctuary occupied the very center of their camp to represent God's presence in the center of their lives. No matter what they faced, they were never without God's presence. Never beyond his reach. Never out of his sight. They learned that God could see everything

Finding sanctuary isn't about what we can do; it's about who God is.

because he was always with them as his manifested presence filled the newly constructed tabernacle.

All of this foreshadowed the day when the glory of God would come to earth and dwell among his people as one of them. As the disciple John described it, "The Word became flesh and dwelt among us" (John 1:14). This is what God has done. He has come to dwell with his people. And now, on this side of the cross, he indwells believers with his Spirit. This means that even today, though we don't have a visible cloud by day or a pillar of fire by night, we still have God's presence with us.

Always.

No matter how hard our days might be, no matter how much we're struggling, no matter what we may be going through, God sees us. He knows more about our circumstance than we do. And he cares. He really, really cares. Even when we can't see his fingerprints on our situation, he is there. Even when we can't see how our current mess could be redeemed, he is there. Even when we feel completely alone in a sea of chaos, he is there. He is always there.

When we believe this to be true about our God—when we really believe it in the marrow of our bones—we don't feel so compelled to cast our cares at the feet of the world. Instead, we cast our cares on him who cares for us because God alone can truly see us.

Turning to a God Who Sees

Scripture affirms this reality in the story of Hagar, a servant girl who was deeply mistreated and sent away. She was alone in her grief when the angel of the Lord appeared to her and spoke words of true comfort to her. In response, Hagar said, *You are the God of seeing!* (Genesis 16:13).

If we serve God who sees us, why do we sometimes feel compelled to take our cares to anyone other than him? And if we serve the God who has brought us into his forever family, why do we sometimes seek words of comfort from people we don't actually dwell in community with? Well, if you're anything like me, sometimes your sin-stained heart will tempt you to look for small comforts in digital spaces, and in the process you end up adding to the noise.

But there is a place we can go, and there is a person we can turn to. Because finding sanctuary isn't about what we can do; it's about who God is. We find sanctuary in his presence. He is the one we turn to when life is turning our world inside out. He is the one we run to when we need someone who will lean in and listen as we pour out our hearts in tears and frustration. And he is the one who has provided us with a family who can surround us in both good times and bad.

The psalms model this for us repeatedly. In Psalm 94:19, we read, "When I am filled with cares, your comfort brings me joy." Oh, that we would bring the cares of our hearts to him who sees us and whose comfort brings us joy.

TUNING IN TO QUIET

Contemplate

1. When you need a few words of encouragement, where do you turn? List as many possibilities as you can think of.
2. After making your list of go-to sources for encouraging words, sort that list into three categories: people, places, and digital spaces. Where do you tend to go the most for encouragement?

3. Read Psalm 94:19 several times. How have you come to know God in his word as a source of comfort and encouragement?

Cultivate

When habits are formed, we do things without even thinking about them. Today, let's change that. Let's plan where we will turn for words of encouragement. There's nothing wrong with reading some positive words on Instagram. Nor is there anything wrong with enjoying the latest inspirational email that lands in our inbox. But let's place three key Bible verses on our phone that we will go to *first* when we need encouragement. Perhaps use a notes app, or if you're going solely analog, use a regular ole' index card. Write down your three favorite encouraging Bible verses. And if you're not sure which ones to go with, pick any three verses you find in this book or look up these and start here: Psalm 121:1-2; Isaiah 41:10; Romans 15:13.

Pray

Lord, we are so grateful that when you speak encouragement over us, your words have staying power. When you say you see us, you really do. You know our situations better than we ever could. Even before we utter a word on our lips, you already know what we need, and you have promised to go before us. We need never worry about what may lie ahead because you are already there. And in you we find rest. We thank you and praise you. In your awesome name, Jesus, we pray. Amen.

Day 11

A DIFFERENT CHOICE ON A DIFFERENT DAY

"... a time to be silent and a time to speak."

Ecclesiastes 3:7

A couple of years ago, I needed surgery in my abdominal area. It was a girl surgery that wasn't supposed to be a big deal. I was supposed to lie low for a couple of weeks and not exercise for about six weeks. Then everything was expected to be fine. But that's not what happened. One week after the surgery, I went in for a follow-up appointment, and I didn't feel right. I was having a hard time breathing, and I was in a lot of pain.

My surgeon requested a CT scan of my lungs, which revealed multiple pulmonary embolisms—blood clots in both of my lungs. This complication from surgery led to an ultra-sound that showed I had deep-vein thrombosis: a blood clot in my leg. Apparently the clot started in my leg and then some smaller clots broke off and traveled to my lungs and lodged themselves there. I didn't know much about blood clots at the time, but I learned pretty quickly that they can be life threatening if not treated. I was immediately admitted to the hospital.

The Pictures I Almost Shared

Sequestered in a hospital room, I was tempted to find my people online. I thought about taking some pictures with my phone. You know the kind. In typical Instagram fashion, I could have taken a picture of my feet at the end of my hospital bed, wearing hospital-issue socks. I could have snapped a shot of the large IV needles stuck in each of my arms, along with the many bruises that had developed almost instantaneously. Or I could have taken a picture of the monitor that hovered above my head with blinking digital numbers that represented my dangerously low oxygen levels and much-too-high heart rate.

Such pictures would have produced a dramatic effect, and in our modern-day culture it's especially alluring to capture every moment of high drama and post it online for all the world to see. Few things garner more attention than posting on social media that you're in a life-or-death situation. I suppose I could have shared a picture and asked for prayer. That would have been reasonable enough, but the words from the Preacher-Poet in Ecclesiastes rang clearly in my heart: "Let your words be few" (Ecclesiastes 5:2). Not only had my ability to speak been more or less taken from me, due to the clots in my lungs impairing my breathing, but I also felt constrained to remain quiet online, too.

My husband contacted our family, our pastor, our small group, and the ladies in my weekly Tuesday evening Bible study. We were well-covered in prayer, not to mention well-fed with casseroles by the people we mixed with regularly in our local church, and my husband provided the necessary updates for them through email. For me, however, I sensed God calling me to a quiet place alone with him. That's where

The words from the Preacher-Poet in Ecclesiastes rang clearly in my heart: “Let your words be few.”

I needed to be, knowing that God alone can give breath and sustain life, so I put my phone away.

Over the next few days, weeks, and months, my "online silence" didn't lead to any spiritual fireworks or a new grandiose vision of God. Instead, my journey to recovery was a slow, plodding one. And yet, God was faithful in those quiet hours that filled each day. As I met with God in his word, he met me in ways no one else could, and in time, he restored my lungs and my breath.

I'm not writing this to say we should never share anything online. It can have its place in our lives, but it is so easy for us to slip into the patterns of the world, adopting the new norms as if there are no ramifications to consider. We can quickly assume the same posture we find others adopting online: sharing—and oversharing—the kinds of stories from our personal lives that are really best shared in the context of a local community, especially our local church.

I don't know what you may be going through right now. Maybe you're in a good place, or maybe you're in a hard place. Wherever you are today, I want to encourage you to seek God in his holy sanctuary. Learn more about him through his word. And dwell with him among his people, because when those hard days come, and they do eventually come for us all, we will know where to turn for true comfort—to the one who sees it all.

TUNING IN TO QUIET

Contemplate

1. When it comes to online sharing, what kinds of stories do you most often find in your feed? Do you notice any patterns?

2. Has there ever been a time in your life when you felt constrained to remain quiet about a specific situation? If so, what were the challenges and what were the blessings that came from being quiet about it? If not, what kinds of scenarios can you think of where it might be wise to refrain from broadcasting the details of a particular situation?
3. As much as this book emphasizes the beauty of cultivating a quiet heart at rest in God's presence, it's also important to have those flesh-and-blood people in your life who you can share your life with, especially when times are hard. Who are those go-to people in your life?

Cultivate

The people I know I can turn to when life gets hard I call my "casserole friends." They're the ones who will bring a casserole—or any kind of meal—when life gets topsy-turvy. The quiet life is not meant to be a solitary life. Just the opposite. We can have a quiet heart precisely because we are surrounded by God's people in both good times and bad. Who can you be a "casserole friend" to today? They don't have to be in a life-and-death situation—just someone who would be blessed to receive a simple meal. And, seriously, it doesn't have to be anything fancy. When I was recovering from surgery, one friend came to my house and brought me a burrito from Taco Bell. It was awesome.

Pray

Lord, we are so grateful that when life hits hardest, you are there. We can always turn to you, and you are faithful to meet us right where we are. Thank you that we never have to face a difficult season on our own, for you are always with us, and you have placed us in your family. We don't need to turn to the right or the left. We can look to you, for you are the God of all comfort. We thank you and praise you, for you are the giver and sustainer of breath. In your powerful name, Jesus, we pray. Amen.

Day 12

THE HANDS THAT SERVE

"Peter got up and went with them. When he arrived, they led him to the room upstairs. And all the widows approached him, weeping and showing him the robes and clothes that Dorcas had made while she was with them."

Acts 9:39

I've always had ugly hands. When I was little—maybe five or six—I admired my big brother's hamster and begged to hold her, but he wouldn't let me. So, I crept into his bedroom one day and took his hamster out of her cage. I sat on the floor to pet her, but she furiously clawed at my hands to get away. I tried not to scream or cry because I didn't want to get caught, but the pain proved too strong. My hands never fully recovered.

I was also born with a nasty wart on my left hand, right where a wedding ring should go. The wart spawned new ones, which concerned the doctor, so he burned them off. But the scars remained. As a high-school student, I once sat in geometry class and passed math papers to the boy behind me. He pointed to my hands and said much too loudly, "You have grandma hands!" I knew he was right. With all the scars and blotches, my hands looked aged.

To this day, I hide my hands inside long sleeves. While some of the old scars have healed, they've been replaced with new ones. I recently had a patch of skin removed from the back of my right hand. Skin cancer. And so it goes. I'll never have pretty hands. If someone tries to take my picture, I instantly put my hands behind me. I want to hide these hideous features, but they are ever before me. Because I'm a writer, they're in front of me always. Whenever I pause to think about a word or phrase, I see them poised on the keys, wrinkled and waiting. It's a great irony to me that I work with ugly hands in the hopes of making something beautiful.

Deep inside all of us, we long to create or build something beautiful. Maybe for you the work of your hands flourishes in the realm of the creative arts. Or maybe the work of your hands thrives in other settings, such as growing a business or raising a family. Maybe you're more like my daughters, who have lovely, graceful hands. Or maybe you're more like me, and you prefer to hide your hands whenever possible. In either case, whether we consider ourselves to have beautiful hands or not, it's the work of our hands that matters most. So, we're left with the question: what will we do with the hands we're given?

To Work with Our Hands

To work with our hands is a biblical principle with significant precedent. In Genesis, God was a gardener. In the New Testament, Jesus was a carpenter. For the Thessalonian believers, however, a curious pattern had developed whereby some of the believers decided to quit working, do nothing with their hands, and live off the generosity of others (2 Thessalonians 3:6-12). They based their decision on Paul's teaching that Christ would soon return and take them home to eternity, but they

To work with our hands—to engage in the physical world God created—is part of God's good design, and it brings him glory when it's done with a heart of obedience and joy.

misunderstood Paul's intention. So, Paul wrote his letter, in part, to correct this false notion. Genuine Christ-followers are not to sit idly by while waiting for Christ to return. As believers, we are to live and work and be a light in the world.

This is why, when Paul said, "seek to lead a quiet life, [and] … mind your own business," he also added, "and … work with your own hands" (1 Thessalonians 4:11-12.) Paul wanted Christ-followers to be responsible workers, but it's notable that he didn't simply say, *Hey, you should get a job.* Instead, he said they should work with their hands. What are we to make of this added admonition? What does working with our hands have to do with leading a quiet life? And what about those who don't necessarily work with their hands as much as their minds, like in the finance industry or digital media?

The Hellenistic culture in which the Thessalonians lived was steeped in classical Greek thought, which considered it more noble to work with your mind than your hands, so Paul wanted to challenge this way of thinking. He wanted to dispel the idea that manual labor was somehow beneath mental labor, and he practiced what he preached. While Paul proclaimed the gospel and wrote vocationally, he supported himself financially by working as a tentmaker—a task that could only be performed by working with his hands (Acts 18:1-3).

This isn't to say that Paul raised manual labor above mental labor; rather, Paul equated all work as worthy of respect. By doing this, Paul not only dignified all work; he also challenged the status quo of his day, which sought to elevate a form of disembodied work.

That Old Divide

In many ways, that old divide still exists. The schism in antiquity, between the philosophical mind and the physiological body, parallels today's schism between disembodied digitalism and the analog world. With the advent of the internet and a host of digital media along with it, we live in a world where many of us work in "knowledge fields," and we may even work remotely. My husband and I are no exception. We both require a laptop to do our jobs, so the answer isn't to reject the digital world and conform to a Luddite existence. But we are wise to recognize the ways in which the world seeks to celebrate disembodied work-lives as somehow superior.

Moreover, when we consider how much the digital realm contributes to the elevated noise levels in this age, it is especially wise to be aware of our own propensity toward all things digital. How much am I participating in this digital age of noise? Are my hands busily preparing my next post? Or do my hands busy themselves more with real-world activities?

In Scripture there's a short but sweet passage that mentions a woman named Dorcas. She was a disciple who was full of "good works and acts of charity" (Acts 9:36). When she became ill and passed away, those around her were deeply grieved, so they sent for Peter. Upon Peter's arrival, everyone kept showing him the "robes and clothes that Dorcas had made" with her hands (v 39). Dorcas made a huge impact on her community through the work of her hands. She served others in the most practical of ways—by making clothes for people. This was the work of her hands. When I think of the work of my own hands, I am reminded of how these not-so-pretty hands of mine have held and rocked and fed my babies. They've scrubbed and scoured sinks and counters. They've tied shoes and brushed hair. They've taken temperatures and measured medicine. They've carried in groceries to feed my family. They've signed countless permission slips for field trips. And they've gripped a steering wheel for hours, to taxi my kids to practices and games.

My hands, though never pretty, have done some pretty amazing things, and I bet the same is true of you. To work with our hands—to engage in the physical world God created—is part of God's good design, and it brings him glory when it's done with a heart of obedience and joy. This doesn't mean we need to quit our desk jobs or start a hands-on hobby, but it does mean that in an electronic age, we must be diligent to seek out ways in which we can embrace the physical world and make it a part of our weekly rhythms. As part of cultivating a quiet life, we are grounded in a very real sense when we intentionally step away from the digital world and embrace the physical world by working with our hands, especially to serve others, on a regular basis.

TUNING IN TO QUIET

Contemplate

1. Have you ever received a handmade gift that someone poured their heart into making? Why are handmade gifts extra special?
2. What kinds of things do you like to create or do with your hands? What kinds of hands-on activities or hobbies would you like to be able to do if you have the time and resources to learn how?
3. Why is working with our hands an important part of leading a quiet life?

Cultivate

Maybe for you the work of your hands is the way you make things for others. This could be meals or baked goods, quilts or scarves. It could be the produce you grow in your garden or the picture frames you make as a craft. Or maybe cooking and crafting aren't your thing. Whether we consider ourselves "crafty" or not, there are countless ways we can serve others with the work of our hands. Maybe you love to make music or poetry, and this is one way you enjoy blessing others. Or maybe you're good at accounting, and you like to help the single moms in your church file their taxes. Or maybe you like to drive, and you're happy giving a lift to some of the seniors in your neighborhood who can't drive anymore. There are countless ways in which we can offer the work of our hands as a gift to others. Today, think of one way you can be a blessing to someone else simply through the work of your hands, whether it's through making something or serving in some way.

Pray

Lord, thank you for the hands you have given us. May the work of our hands bring delight to those around us and glory to your name. Whenever we feel pulled into a purely digital type of activity, help us not to linger there too long; rather, help us to intentionally re-engage with your beautiful world in helpful, tangible ways. We ask this in your beautiful name, Jesus. Amen.

Day 13

WHEN SMALL THINGS MATTER IN BIG WAYS

"Then Jesus then took the loaves, and after giving thanks he distributed them to those who were seated—so also with the fish, as much as they wanted."

John 6:11

The seeds in my hand felt like tiny specks of near-nothingness. And yet, after I planted them in good soil, they grew into tall and brilliant zinnias despite my notorious black thumb. Day by day I watched those zinnias with wonder, knowing I didn't have much to do with their zealous growth. I may have planted the small seeds, but God and nature did the rest.

I think it's like that with just about anything we put our hand to. We offer the small bit we have; then we sit back and watch God take it from there. Like the boy with a lunch sack of five barley loaves and two fish. In the boy's hands, they were mere loaves and fishes, but in Jesus' hands, they became a feast for the multitude (John 6:1-13). This is true with anything we might do. God takes our small contribution and makes something glorious.

The Women Who Worked with Their Hands

When God's people set about constructing the tabernacle-sanctuary in the wilderness, the women had a small but important task at hand. Moses writes, "And all the women whose hearts were moved spun the goat hair by virtue of their skill" (Exodus 35:26). I don't know how to spin goat hair, and nothing about it seems especially important. But I learned that a goat has two coats of hair, with the coarser hair on top and the softer down underneath. This softer hair is made of small fibers that can be twisted together to create a luxurious yarn.

Today, this is what cashmere is made of, but in biblical times, this yarn was used for a lot of things. The women in the wilderness worked with their hands to make the yarn; then they dyed it red, blue, and purple. These threads were then used to make the priestly garments, as well as the veil that separated the Holy Place from the Most Holy Place.

Moses's commendation of these women who committed themselves to such tedious work is encouraging because this passage reflects how God can use us, whatever our skills may be, for his glory. It doesn't matter how small or obscure the work of our hands might seem. God loves to invite his daughters to use their skills for his kingdom.

One of the ways we cultivate a quiet heart in a noisy and demanding world is by working with our hands. Whether we use our hands to serve others or to make something tangible, we can offer the work of our hands as a gift to God, for him to use however he wishes. Ultimately, the impact of the work of our hands is never up to us. It's always up to God. Our part is simple obedience: to do that which he has called us to do. God loves to take small things and make them matter in big ways.

God loves to take small things and make them matter in big ways.

Never before have Paul's words, to "work with your hands," been more needed. Rather than trying to build something big for ourselves, which usually involves a lot of loud work, we can be content quietly doing whatever God has placed in front of us, even the small things. Because small things can make big impacts.

Christianity, of course, is founded upon the incarnation—the very premise that God the Son took on the form of embodied flesh as a small baby. Few things are smaller than a baby, and yet, he came as a tiny human so he could dwell among us and eventually give his life for us. And from the earliest pages of Scripture, the incarnation of God was foreshadowed in the sanctuary.

The colors of the veil in the sanctuary—made from the hands of women in the wilderness—I believe hinted at the future incarnation of God. Since the color of the sky is blue, I like to think that the blue threads in the veil represented the heavens, which reflect Christ's deity. And since the color of blood is red, I wonder if the scarlet threads in the veil represented Christ's humanity. As blue and scarlet are combined, the color purple is formed, which is the color of royalty. Then, the very moment Jesus died on the cross, the veil in the later-built temple was torn in two, and, it seems to me, the very threads representing Christ's deity and humanity were torn just as his flesh had been torn.

The rent veil means we now have access to the very presence of God, which was formerly accessed only once a year by the high priest. Now, we are invited to enter in.

Everything about that old tabernacle-sanctuary pointed to Jesus. A craftsman named Bezalel and his team worked with their hands to build it. The women worked with their hands to weave fine linen for it. And once it was finished, the priests then worked with their hands to bring daily sacrifices to the bronze altar. Their work wasn't pretty. In fact, it was bloody work. But it was a necessary part of why the tabernacle was there. All of it pointed to the day when God would come to dwell among his people as one of them and hold in his hands the gift of salvation to all who believe.

The Hands That Heal

When I think about the hands of God, I think about the tiny hands that cupped the face of his young mother. The growing hands that learned the trade of his stepfather. The compassionate hands that touched the sick and dying. And the tender hands that broke the bread and gave thanks.

Then, one Friday, the hands that once shaped timber allowed a wooden cross to reshape his. Pierced, his hands bled. Three days later, those once-dead hands held the grace which the whole world needs. But the scars remained. His friend Thomas touched them, to confirm it was really him. Today, those same scarred hands offer the healing every human soul desperately needs.

This is the work of God's hands.

The actual sanctuary in the Old Testament served to point people to our day, when we can look to Christ as our sanctuary. It is the work of Christ's scarred hands that replaces the ashes of our lives with the beauty of him. And in him, we find rest from the loud and clamorous world around us. Then, as we work with our hands to serve others, Christ takes our few "loaves and fishes," and he turns them into a grand feast. He takes our small contributions and turns them into beautiful blessings for others.

What you do matters. The meals you make. The friends you visit. The cards you write. The kids you bathe. The flowers you plant. The songs you sing. The stories you tell. The bread you bake. The walks you take. The words you speak. The smiles you share. The gifts you give. All of it matters. Because the small things in our hands become big things in God's hands.

TUNING IN TO QUIET

Contemplate

1. How has someone been a blessing to you by doing a small thing that mattered to you in a big way?
2. What are some of the small things you enjoy doing for others?
3. How is leading a quiet life one small way in which we can point to our big God?

Cultivate

In a world that likes to lavish praise on big things, a person leading a quiet life finds solace in small things, knowing that all things matter to God, and that in his hands, our small things become his big things. Today, identify one small way in which you can consistently contribute good things to others. This could be something you're already doing, like showing up at work and placing encouraging post-it notes on coworkers' desks or offering to watch a friend's child who has special needs. Pick a small thing that you either do already or would like to start doing, and let that be "your thing."

Pray

Lord, thank you that nothing we do is ever too small or too unimportant for you. In fact, you love to take our small offerings and use them in big ways. It's what you do. Over and over again. Thank you for the sweet privilege of allowing the work of our hands to be used in ways that can be a blessing to others. Help us to remember that the work of our hands is never about us but always about the good work that you are bringing about, day in and day out. We love you, Lord, In your magnificent name, Jesus, we pray. Amen.

Day 14

THE QUESTION WE MUST SETTLE

"Your word is a lamp for my feet and a light on my path."

Psalm 119:105

One year when I worked as a schoolteacher, a young coworker pitched an idea to everyone in our department. Inspired by a picture she found online, she thought it would be cool if each of us dressed up on Halloween according to our favorite social-media platform. She said the 20-somethings on our team could dress up as Snapchat and TikTok. The 30-somethings could dress like Instagram and YouTube. The 40-somethings could have Facebook and Twitter. And the one 50-something on our team? MySpace.

The younger team members loved the idea. The rest of us sort of stared at one another in confusion. For starters, we weren't sure how one might dress up as a social-media platform, but a few pictures from Pinterest showed a group of teachers at another school where each teacher wore a different colored t-shirt with a social-media logo on the front. For instance, the teacher representing Facebook wore a blue t-shirt with Facebook's white "f" logo; the young woman representing Snapchat wore a yellow t-shirt with Snapchat's logo, and so forth. To accessorize her outfit, Facebook girl added glittery blue fairy wings, a blue halo made of tinsel, and a blue tutu. The rest did likewise.

I haven't worn a tutu since I was eight and didn't feel much inclined to wear one now, but deeper implications concerned me. I didn't feel comfortable promoting social media to minors. Study after study has linked the harmful effects of social media on young people's mental health, so this celebration of social media in our classrooms seemed inappropriate. But this is the world we live in now—a world where even the adults are jumping on a noisy bandwagon to parade social media down the hallways of our schools.

It's possible I was overthinking it. Perhaps it was all just for fun. But then again, if we want to cultivate a quiet life and be an instrument of peace for those around us, we must be clear about the sources of true authority in our lives. It all comes down to influence. Who do we want to influence us? Do we want the voices with selfies on social media to be our main sources of influence? Or do we want the voices of those we actually live with and fellowship with—those who really know us—to influence us?

We may think social media isn't really influencing us, and perhaps we simply scroll for fun sometimes. But social media isn't neutral. Even secular news outlets like the *New York Times* acknowledge as much.[10] The primary goal of every social-media platform is to capture as much of our attention as possible. And since we become what we behold, we must be diligent about the things we give our attention to.

"As We Commanded You"

Tucked inside that signature verse about leading a quiet life is a little phrase where Paul says, "… as we commanded you." Paul urges believers then and today "to seek to lead a quiet life,

It is impossible to lead a quiet life in a world bent on deception and destruction if we are not regularly submitting ourselves to the final authority of God's word.

to mind your own business, and to work with your hands, as we commanded you" (1 Thessalonians 4:11). Who was Paul to tell anybody what to do? Well, he devoted a fair amount of ink to telling the story of how Jesus called him to proclaim the gospel (Galatians 1:11-24). Today, the church rightly recognizes his apostolic authority to write down words of truth as he was inspired by the Holy Spirit, and he wasn't the only one. God had used several dozen of his faithful followers to inscribe the words of Old Testament Scripture over the course of approximately 2,000 years, as well as using several other followers of Jesus to write New Testament Scripture. We live in a time, though, that seeks to question all authority.

The spirit of this age tries to convince us that nobody can tell us what is right or wrong, and the world says we need to look inside ourselves to find truth. But as followers of Christ, we look to the Bible as the source of all truth (1 Peter 1:10-12). Indeed, Jesus is truth (John 14:6). The riches of God's word are timeless in goodness, truth, and beauty. It is impossible to lead a quiet life in a world bent on deception and destruction if we are not regularly submitting ourselves to the final authority of God's word.

For every one of us, we must settle the question: *who has ultimate authority in my life?* For me, I look to the Bible as the final authority in my life. That doesn't mean I always live up perfectly to everything it says, but when I fail—and I fail plenty—I ask for forgiveness and keep forging ahead by God's grace.

The Bible is an active living force in my life (Hebrews 4:12), shaping the way I think and the way I view myself and the world around me. Sure, there are some strange passages in the ancient text, but I've settled the matter in my heart: if there's something in the Bible I don't understand at first, I work through it patiently until I do, and God is always faithful to reveal himself through his word. The more I learn about God, the more I know I can trust him.

It's no surprise that inside the tabernacle-sanctuary, and inside the Most Holy Place, and inside the ark of the covenant, lay the stone tablets with the Ten Commandments. God's commands were not restrictive bounds to prevent people from having fun, but they were God-designed boundaries that gave life. And the same is true of his commands today.

The psalmist describes God's word as a lamp for our feet, for it guides us and shows us our next steps. But our natural inclination is to bristle against anyone who "commands" anything of us. And yet, whenever we veer off on our own paths, we end up in a mud pit of our own making. Have you ever been there? I know I have, and I've learned this to be true: God's word is authoritative precisely because it speaks life. It shows us how best to live life to the fullest.

I sincerely wrestled with whether to participate with my team at work, so on the day in question, I wore a t-shirt with a stack of books on the front. I didn't want to be a party pooper. But social media? That was furthest from the thing I wanted to promote in my classroom. Social media is like a noisy gong with humans clanging for attention. I wanted to lead by example, showing that there are a better founts to drink from. There are books aplenty, and one especially with genuine authority to proclaim what is good and true and beautiful.

TUNING IN TO QUIET

Contemplate

1. Have you ever bristled against someone who "commanded" you to do something? What happened? Why is it in our nature to reject authority?
2. Why is it important that a person in authority be a person who is both humble and wise, as well as someone who genuinely wants what is best for us?
3. How have you settled this question: who has ultimate authority in your life?

Cultivate

Consider the various authority figures in your life over the years. For most of us, we'd say those were our parents, pastors, teachers, and bosses. Who else would you add to this list? After looking over your own list, honestly ask yourself where you would place God's word on that list. What might it "cost" you to submit to God's word as the final authority in your life? What might you gain?

Pray

Lord, thank you that we can always look to you as the one true source of authority in our lives. You have not left us without a guide or a guidebook. Help us to continually submit to your word as the ultimate authority in our lives; and when we fail, it is your kindness that leads us to repentance. We thank you that you are good and your word will never fail us. In your truth-filled name, Jesus, we pray. Amen.

Day 15

OF COMFORT AND CONVICTION

"Blessed be the God and Father of our Lord Jesus Christ, the Father of mercies and the God of all comfort. He comforts us in all our affliction, so that we may be able to comfort those who are in any kind of affliction, through the comfort we ourselves receive from God."

2 Corinthians 1:3-4

I understand why social media is so magnetizing. A popular trend in the online space is to produce words that bring comfort. Don't we all want comfort? I know I do. I'm all about comfort. I like wrapping up in a plush chenille blanket, while drinking a hot cup of tea and reading an old book. I also appreciate comfort in the form of stretchy yoga pants, even though I never do yoga. And it's not just these simple comforts I enjoy. I welcome the comfort that comes with predictable routines, and I especially relish the comfort of being around like-hearted people who totally get me.

All that is to say I am probably not much different than the average online reader, looking for comfort in the words I read.

And yet...

Comfort isn't my only aim in life. After all, the Bible isn't always comforting to read. I mean, it's easy enough to cherry-pick the "happy verses" that tell us how we're made in God's image and loved by him, all of which are true. But there are other passages where the author's primary purpose isn't necessarily to bring comfort but to bring conviction.

The Truest Comfort There Is

I dare say conviction may be going out of style these days. It is far easier—and far more popular—to tell people how amazing they are, how loved they are, and how great they are as moms or friends or whatever. This kind of ultra-positivity is everywhere, both within Christian spheres and without.

On the one hand, I'll take the positivity over the negativity that is also pervasive on the internet. On the other hand, just as a steady diet of sugary sweets cannot nourish the body, a steady word-diet of sweet positivity cannot nourish the soul. We need the substance of truth.

As online readers, though, we like comfort, and at times, tender comfort may be exactly what is needed in a particular moment. But we will never grow into the fullness of maturity if we subsist solely on an intake of sweet, comforting words. We need truth—the kind of truth that can only be found in Scripture. For instance, the Bible says that in the heavenly sanctuary, every hour of every day, there are creatures saying, "Holy, holy, holy, Lord God, the Almighty" (Revelation 4:8).

When I consider the holiness of God, I am also convicted of my own unholiness. God is holy; I am not. This is a fundamental premise in the story of redemption and the reason why we cannot enter the sanctuary of his presence without the sacrifice Christ made on the cross. We need Christ to save us precisely because we cannot acquire holiness on our own. I appreciate how one author expounded on this:

> *Repetition is a form of emphasis … The Bible never says that God is love, love, love; or mercy, mercy, mercy; or wrath, wrath, wrath; or justice, justice, justice. It does say that He is holy, holy, holy.*[11]

If you are in a place where you desperately need some words of comfort, I am convinced that the totality of Scripture offers the truest comfort one can find anywhere, and it's this: God is holy, holy, holy. I am not, not, not. I am a sinner—completely unable to produce any kind of holiness or goodness in myself.

In my darkest days, I needed rescuing, and to God's amazing glory, he saved me. He lifted me out of a miry pit of despair and gave me new life. And he will do the same for you, which is the truest comfort there is. So, I'm not saying I think comfort should go out of style. Not at all. The apostle Paul described God as "the God of all comfort [who] comforts us in all our affliction, so that we may be able to comfort those who are in any kind of affliction, through the comfort we ourselves receive from God." (2 Corinthians 1:3-4). Genuine comfort is a beautiful thing, but so is honest conviction.

One of the ways we cultivate a quiet heart is by accepting the Holy Spirit's conviction when we read the words of Scripture. It's interesting that Jesus never said, *Comfort will set you free.* He said, "The truth will set you free" (John 8:32). And that, my friends, is what I want for all of us—to know the truth that sets us free. Nothing could be more comforting than that.

TUNING IN TO QUIET

Contemplate

1. What are some of your favorite comforts?
2. How would you explain to a friend the difference between words of comfort and words of conviction? How is conviction different than condemnation?
3. How have you known God as the greatest comforter?

Cultivate

To have a quiet heart that knows God's peace is to have a heart-posture that welcomes God's conviction as a means of grace. His conviction is never punitive but restorative, which is why we can receive it gladly, knowing that it's for our good. One of the ways in which we can position ourselves to be more receptive to God's instructive correction in our lives is with our posture when we pray. When we bow or kneel, we demonstrate with our bodies that we are yielding to God's authority in our lives. Likewise, when we pray with open hands, we assume a posture that is willing to receive whatever God gives, trusting that his gifts are ultimately for our good, even if we require some pruning in the meantime. Today, practice one or more of these postures when you pray the following prayer.

Pray

Lord, thank you for both the comfort and the conviction that you bring through your word. Help us to embrace both as necessary for growing into the fullness of maturity in Christ. And when those around us are hurting, may we offer the same comfort to others that you have so generously given to us—for it is only in you that we find the truest comfort for our souls. In your comforting and convicting name, Jesus, we pray. Amen.

Day 16

KNOWN BY LOVE

"Choose for yourselves today: Which will you worship … As for me and my family, we will worship the L*ORD."*

Joshua 24:15

In my house I have a writing room. I suppose you could call it a home office, but that sounds so office-like. This is my prayer room and quiet room and book room. In truth, it's my own little sanctuary, complete with a tiny pew I found, in distressed antique white. My little pew is a simple wooden bench with a few white pillows, and next to it I have placed one of my all-time favorite novels called *The Remains of the Day* by Kazuo Ishiguro. It's there as a reminder.

Set in rural England, the novel depicts an aging butler, Stevens, who manages the household affairs of a once prestigious estate. Like the antiquated manor, Stevens finds himself in a modernized world that views butlers as mere relics of the past. Thanks to advancing technology, there are now more expedient ways of polishing the silver and buffing the floors, so the butler is facing a world that continues to change around him as it sends the not-so-subtle message that he isn't really needed anymore.

In the final scene, Stevens sits on a bench at the end of a pier, watching the sun descend into the ocean's abyss. Just as evening is on its way, so his final years of life are also fast approaching. Stevens must ask himself: What remains of his day? What will he do with the time he's been given? What does he want to be remembered for?

These are questions we are wise to ask ourselves as well. What will we do with the time we've been given? What do we want to be remembered for?

Why We Are Here

While we're here, we're to live as lights pointing to the one true Light of the world, and one way we do this is by cultivating a quiet life. We examine our heart's motives and ambitions. We retrain our focus on what truly edifies. We enjoy the work of our hands as a means to serve others. And we do all of this as we immerse ourselves in the authoritative truth of God's word. These are just some of the more practical measures we can take toward cultivating a quiet heart in a noisy and demanding world, but it's also important to note that these habits are not exhaustive. If anything, they're merely a starting point.

The apostle Paul says in another letter that we're to "put on love," which binds all the virtues together in perfect unity (Colossians 3:14). Love is like the undercurrent in all we do. In fact, this passage we've been examining in 1 Thessalonians is prefaced with Paul's admonition for those believers to continue loving others as they had been (1 Thessalonians 4:9-10), because without love, we're just noisy gongs and clanging cymbals, which is the very opposite of a quiet life (1 Corinthians 13:1).

In the end, it boils down to this: we will be known and remembered by how well we love others. Not by how many likes we get on our latest TikTok video. Not by how many

In the end, it boils down to this: we will be known and remembered by how well we love others.

followers we amass on Twitter. And not for how many emojis we gather on Instagram. We will be known for our love.

We are called to love others, and the best way to show our love is to be present, in the flesh, with those around us. This is why the Son of God came: to show us his love for us by coming to dwell among us. He could have stayed in heaven and sent us messages or memes. In fact, over many centuries, God did send his messengers, but humans rejected his message. Then he came himself by sending his Son, Jesus, to love us with his presence. And this is how we show love to others—with our presence. Jesus summed it up nicely when he said, "By this everyone will know that you are my disciples, if you love one another" (John 13:35).

Rather than the siren call of the social-media scroll, we respond to the clarion call of the gospel, which invites us to participate with God in restoring the world and its inhabitants by sharing his grace as we yield to the time-tested instructions given to us through Scripture. And we do this by loving those around us with our physical presence.

Our God-Given Purpose

The character of Stevens, the aging English butler, reminds me of Joshua, another servant facing the end of his life. When Joshua spoke to the nation of Israel for the last time, he said, "Choose for yourselves today: Which will you worship? … As for me and my family, we will worship the Lord" (Joshua 24:15). This particular translation uses the word "worship," which is interesting because many translations use the word "serve." The connection is clear. We worship what we serve. The aging butler in the novel devoted his life to serving one master at a grand estate, only to realize later that his master was, in fact, a Nazi sympathizer.

All of us must choose who we will serve. I don't want to be like Stevens and get to the end of my life and regret the choices I made and the master I served. I want to be a servant like Joshua, who braved treacherous waters and faced giant enemies but entered the promised land anyway. For us, the promised land is eternity with Christ as he makes a new heaven and a new earth. But for now, we can wake each day and ask God to help us love each soul he brings across our path. This is our God-given purpose.

Every morning in my writing room, I sit on my tiny pew, like a small prayer bench, and I ask God to show me how I can love others better—because this quiet life isn't about what we can gain for ourselves as much as it's about living as a witness to those around us, just as the Israelites with the sanctuary in their midst were supposed to live as a testimony to the nations around them.

When Paul tells believers "to seek to lead a quiet life, to mind your own business, and to work with your own hands, as we commanded you," he also adds, "so that you may behave properly in the presence of outsiders" (1 Thessalonians 4:11-12). This connotes a life of godly witness, and our witness will be futile without love.

As you wake every morning, I encourage you to find a few quiet moments when you can thank God for the breath he gives and the people he has given to you to love. Then ask him to grow in you a greater love for others. For as we are known by Love himself, let us also be known for our love (1 John 4:19-21).

TUNING IN TO QUIET

Contemplate

1. What are you mostly known for now? In other words, where do you spend most of your time? What do you spend most of your time doing?
2. Ultimately, what do you want to be remembered for?
3. How might our physical presence communicate love for others?

Cultivate

Presence. In the Bible, God's people experienced his presence in his sanctuary. They also experienced it on a mountaintop, in a valley, under a tree, atop the water, and in many other places. It's the same today. We can experience God's presence anywhere we go because he is with us wherever we go. This is one of the primary ways in which God shows his love for us: by being with us. In the same way, we communicate our love for others with our physical presence and intentional focus. Merely being in a room with people while also being absorbed with our phones doesn't communicate love. So, when we are with people—whether they are our family and friends or our coworkers and colleagues—let's put our phones away so we can devote our focus to those around us. In this key way, we can show our love.

Pray

Lord, thank you for each new morning you give us. We know that we are only here by your grace. Help us to grow in our love for others, more and more, so that we may become living testimonies as to how we have been changed by your love—for without your love, we cannot know true love because you are love, and by your love we are able to love others. We thank you and praise you. In your loving name, Jesus, we pray. Amen.

Day 17

THIS IS JUST THE OVERTURE

"For our momentary light affliction is producing for us an absolutely incomparable eternal weight of glory. So we do not focus on what is seen, but on what is unseen. For what is seen is temporary, but what is unseen is eternal."

2 Corinthians 4:17-18

I could feel the tension rising in my neck. It was my own fault, and I knew it. I had said yes to too many commitments, and now I felt that I had no choice but to plow ahead until everything got done. Then the neck pain grew so intense that it forced me to lie in bed and do nothing. My body demanded that I rest. Frustrated by this untimely delay, I called a friend who works as a nurse and explained my plight.

My sweet friend responded matter-of-factly: "Stress always takes a toll on our bodies. It just expresses itself in different ways. Some people have migraines. Others experience indigestion. And others will feel tension in their neck or spasms in their back."

So, basically, I needed less stress in my life. Don't we all? In this journey toward cultivating a quiet heart, we sometimes take two steps forward and then one step back. That's what this neck-induced bedrest felt like: a step back. But even as my body demanded rest, I knew I needed more than a long nap. I needed a different perspective.

When Loud Messages Lead to Restless Hearts

In today's noisy world, one of the loudest messages we hear is "Live your best life now!" or "Live your one life well!" Then we push ourselves hard to make this so-called "one life" a good one, as if everything is up to us. This is at the root of our hustle and striving—to make good things happen for ourselves and to experience as many of those good things as possible while we can. But the underlying theme of this message—that we have only "one life"—is fundamentally untrue.

As believers in the risen Christ, we're not given "one life" on this earth and then that's it: game over. To be a follower of Christ means we are no longer citizens of this world; we are citizens of heaven (Philippians 3:20). This world is not our home. We are pilgrims passing through to a better place. We know this to be true because Jesus himself declared that he was going ahead of us to "prepare a place" for each of his followers (John 14:1-3).

To lead a quiet life is to hold the conviction that this life here and now is not all there is. When our circumstances threaten to unravel us, we are held by the Spirit of God inside us, knowing that no matter what happens, nothing in this world is permanent. A better world, and a better life, awaits. This is the crux of the hope we have because of Christ.

The goal of every believer, then, is to become more like Christ and spend eternity with him, and the quiet life is the way we live out this goal. Far too often, though, we lose sight of this truth as we're inundated with the challenges of daily life. When our days get crazy, we find ourselves living a stressful life instead of a quiet life. That was certainly true of

There's an inner resoluteness that comes from knowing that there is a world beyond this world and that God is completely in control of all of it.

me and the literal pain in my neck, and I think it's true of a lot of us. Thankfully, Scripture provides us with the sure anchor we need whenever the tempest of life swirls around us.

The World Beyond What We Can See

There is so much more to this world than we can see with our eyes. In 2 Kings 6:8-18, the prophet Elisha and his servant are surrounded by an enemy army. They're so outnumbered that anyone with eyes can see they are doomed, which is exactly what the servant sees. But Elisha prays and says, "LORD, please open his eyes and let him see" (v 17). Then the Lord opens the servant's eyes, and he beholds an even greater army of horses and chariots of fire surrounding the enemy army.

This story in the Bible illustrates the reality that there is more to this life than what we can see with our physical eyes. There is a spiritual realm that exists outside of our time-bound world, and this is the world where we are heading. Elisha may have lived a quiet life, but that doesn't mean he was always quiet—quite the opposite, in fact. The very reason the king of Syria and his army wanted to silence Elisha for good was because he kept proclaiming God's truth as an anointed prophet.

You see, the quiet life doesn't mean we refrain from speaking the truth while counting the days until we can quietly go to heaven. The quiet life is really a way of speaking about a person's inner life. There's an inner resoluteness that comes from knowing that there is a world beyond this world and that God is completely in control of all of it. We don't have to stress ourselves out by taking on too many commitments or by saying yes to too many things because we're not going to miss out on anything important. Instead, we can trust that every aspect of our lives is ordered and ordained by God in heaven. We can breathe easy knowing that time isn't running out. We have eternity ahead of us.

A person leading a quiet life walks through each day with eternity in view. Assured. Unflappable. This is what it means to lead a quiet life. It's to live with Spirit-directed eyes, trusting that God has every single detail under his control. Nothing is beyond his reach or his timing.

To cultivate a quiet heart is to embrace the truth that we are sojourners just passing through to a better place, but while we're here, we have a mission to accomplish. We're here to be witnesses to the beauty of God's grace—the grace seen in how he forgives us and wants to welcome us home for eternity in his presence in that heavenly sanctuary.

To Cease All Striving

Hustle-induced stress is really just another human attempt at striving for self-glory. But when we replace our desire for self-glory with a desire to bring God glory, we feel much less inclined to take on too much. Our focus is no longer on ourselves and what we are aiming to accomplish. Instead, our focus is on living for others and being a light.

C.S. Lewis once remarked that "Glory means good report with God."[12] In other words, the glory we should desire most is to hear one day that divine accolade, "Well done, good and faithful servant!" (Matthew 25:23). If this is truly what we aspire to hear one day, then that inner drive to take on too much will dissipate.

The world may tell us to invest our energies into living "our best life now" or "our one life well," but we know this view neglects the eternal reality of our souls (2 Corinthians 4:13-18). To lead a quiet life is to look ahead with Spirit-directed eyes and believe by faith that a better world awaits. For this is where our true hope, true peace, and true confidence are found.

TUNING IN TO QUIET

Contemplate

1. When you are feeling stressed, how does that stress manifest itself in your body?
2. Do you tend to say yes to too many things and take on too many commitments? Why do you think that is?
3. While rest is always helpful, how is a shift in perspective also a necessary part in cultivating a quiet heart? In other words, why is it crucial that quiet hearts see with Spirit-directed eyes that this world is not our home—that we are pilgrims passing through?

Cultivate

Let's practice shifting our perspective. Take a moment and look around you. What do you see? Note your surroundings. Then remind yourself that everything you see is temporal. Then close your eyes and ask God to help you remember that there is so much more than what we can see with our eyes. Today isn't about doing as much as it is about seeing—seeing the things around us and the activities in front of us as temporary things in a temporary world.

Pray

Lord, thank you that we don't have to hustle or strive for anything, as if this life is all there is. This life you've given us is a gift, to be sure, but it is only the overture. There is so much more to look forward to, and we can rest knowing that you have everything under control. Help us to live each day with a quiet heart that longs to hear you say one day, "Well done." We ask this in your sweet name, Jesus. Amen.

Day 18

THE PURSUIT OF LESS

"I have learned to be content in whatever circumstances I find myself."

Philippians 4:11

Along California's central coast lies a castle on a hill. Hearst Castle is open for public tours where you can see how the rich and famous of a past generation once lived. The estate is too large to see in one tour, so several different tours are available. I've only been on one of them, but it sufficed to capture the essence of a lavish lifestyle. The castle has an Olympic-sized outdoor pool that is surrounded by Greek-style columns and statues, a massive dining hall that once served exquisite meals for large parties, and many bedrooms that once hosted guests from Hollywood.

Walking through such a grand place reminded me of the old TV show called *Lifestyles of the Rich and Famous*. We humans are captivated by wealth. What is ordinary for the super well-off is so far outside the norm for us regular folk that we watch in amazement and wonder.

Today, we don't need television or actual tours to give us a glimpse into the lives of the rich and famous. On Instagram, celebrities pull back the curtain and let everyone into their "everyday lives." With their pictures of extravagant vacations, we see them wearing beautiful gowns and visiting exotic places. With their Insta-stories, we see them picking out their clothes inside huge closets or lying by the pool in a backyard that looks more like a luxurious garden.

But when the Snapchat shot is over or the TikTok video ends, we return to the dailyness of our ordinary lives, where we're confronted with a kitchen that doesn't come with a hired chef, a living space that doesn't come with paid housekeepers, and a yard that doesn't come with a landscape architect. This is real life, in which we have to pick up after ourselves and figure out what we're going to prepare for dinner.

The Pursuit of More

It's tempting sometimes to desire more opulent surroundings. A life of luxury and ease sounds enticing. But if we're committed to cultivating a quiet heart, our hearts must be free from the pursuit of more. Now, I'm not talking about basic necessities. We need food and clothing. We need loving relationships and safe dwellings. What I'm talking about is that seedling of discontent inside us that stirs a restlessness  in our soul, for ingratitude is incompatible with a quiet heart. We cannot have a heart at rest when we are constantly yearning for more and more.

To cultivate a quiet heart is to live free from the pursuit of more. It's often through the pursuit of less that we are freed from the talons of material things. This isn't to say that owning things is necessarily bad or wrong, but when our desire for more leads to thanklessness and covetousness, we have entered spiritually dangerous territory. We need to ask ourselves: Do we own our stuff? Or does our stuff own us? Too often it's the latter, and a quiet life is incongruent with a discontented heart.

To cultivate a quiet heart is to live free from the pursuit of more.

Now, you might be wondering about all that gold that was used for the temple, or even that earlier sanctuary, the tabernacle. Why was so much gold a part of the sanctuary? It's true that the few furnishings inside the sanctuary were made of gold. For instance, the lampstand in the Holy Place was made of solid gold, and the table with the bread of presence was made of acacia wood and then overlaid with gold, as was the ark of the covenant inside the Most Holy Place (Exodus 25).

Gold, a pure metal, signified purity, so it was appropriate that the purest and finest of metals be used because it represented the fact that God is holy. Moreover, the gold didn't come from heavy taxes. It came from free-will offerings. The people gave from their abundance, which they plundered from the Egyptians as they left Egypt, and that was brought about through God's hands. So, the people's gifts of gold were really their way of giving back to God what he had first given to them.

God's small original sanctuary wasn't about the gold. It wasn't about being impressive. It was about people entering his holy presence and communing with the one who made us. God was never concerned with his house being elaborate. In fact, the extreme extravagance of the later temple became a big part of Israel's eventual downfall.

When Discontent Leads to Disobedience

Castle tours and private showings have been around a long time. When Solomon reigned as king of Israel, news of his wisdom and wealth spread far and wide. The reports were so extravagant, though, that some wondered if they were a bit exaggerated.

When the queen of Sheba heard the news, she travelled from Egypt to Israel to see for herself if the reports were true.

Her journey across 1,400 miles of desert sands took several months, but when she finally reached the house of Solomon, she saw that everything she had heard wasn't even the half of it (1 Kings 10:1-10). Solomon's wealth was so vast that silver was considered as common as stone in Jerusalem (v 27).

In this story in 1 Kings 10, the word "gold" is mentioned a total of 14 times. This is no coincidence, for the writer of 1 and 2 Kings is composing a historical account of how and why Israel ended up in bondage to Babylon. Through a series of comparisons and contrasts, the writer holds up each king of Israel to God's commands in Deuteronomy, which explicitly state that Israel's king was not to accumulate much wealth (Deuteronomy 17:17).

The biblical account of Solomon's extensive accumulation of wealth is really an indictment against him. Not only that but Solomon used slave labor to build the temple, which showed that Solomon's heart had been wandering from God for some time, for the story of God's redemption is about delivering his people from slavery to freedom, which parallels the spiritual freedom we receive today as a gift of his grace. Solomon's story is one of discontent leading to disobedience, for his fall began with one bad choice followed by another and another, until eventually he turned to idol worship, at which point God decided to tear the kingdom of Israel in two (1 Kings 11:9-13).

Quieting a Room and Quieting Our Hearts

Today, interior designers talk about "quieting a room" by decluttering our spaces from an overabundance of stuff. A room just feels more spacious and, in my opinion, more inviting when there is less visual "noise." In the same way, we can quiet our hearts with greater ease when there are fewer material distractions around us. This doesn't mean we need to become chic minimalists, but we are wise to recognize the way in which clutter—and the way we cling to it—might affect us.

To possess wealth is not wrong, but Scripture is clear that the *love* of money leads to evil (1 Timothy 6:10). So, we must check our hearts for any traces of a disordered desire for more of it. When we are mesmerized by wealth. When we scroll to admire those who have it. When we flaunt what little we have of it. These are warnings signs that something is amiss inside our hearts.

Instead of being impressed with the wealthy lifestyles we see in pictures or videos, let's relinquish the world's pursuit of more and instead embrace the quiet simplicity of our own lives. And let's remember to give thanks for the people we share life with and for the common gifts of grace we receive each day. When we do this, we remain tethered to what is true and what is real, and we grow in contentment for that which we already have. This pursuit of less, in turn, is a key means of growing an inner quietness of heart.

TUNING IN TO QUIET

Contemplate

1. Have you ever toured a mansion or a castle? Do you ever watch those TV shows or Instagram Reels that depict extravagant lifestyles? Why are people naturally drawn to those types of things?
2. In the case of Solomon, why was an overabundance of wealth part of his downfall?
3. The original tabernacle held a few gold furnishings; why do you think God wanted his sanctuary to be relatively free from a multitude of material things?

Cultivate

Part of cultivating a quiet heart is to live in a way that is free from the pursuit of more: to cherish what we already have and to be at rest in a place of deep contentment. It's not wrong to enjoy nice things, but it is important that those things don't occupy a large focus in our lives. To live in pursuit of less, popular online voices will tell us to declutter our homes and count the things we're grateful for, and these aren't bad places to start. But for our hearts to be truly free from the talons of material things, we also need to practice generosity. We need to practice giving, not only to the church but also to others. We need to give not only from our abundance, but we need to give sacrificially, too. Today, prayerfully ask God to bring someone to mind and ask him to show you how you might give away something of yours that you enjoy. Then watch how your gift becomes a blessing to someone else.

Pray

Lord, thank you that you do not look at outward appearances, but you look at our hearts. You are not concerned with how much we have or don't have. You simply want to be in fellowship with us. Forgive us when we are enticed to want more and more. Help us to remain content with everything you have given us, for in you we have all that we need. And help us to live generously, sharing with others what you have already shared with us. We love you and are so grateful for who you are. In your abundant name, Jesus, we pray. Amen.

Day 19

LOSS CAN EITHER DEFINE OR REFINE

"But everything that was a gain to me, I have considered to be a loss because of Christ."

Philippians 3:7

I stood on my porch and watched as a huge moving truck parked in front of our house. The movers then loaded all of our furniture plus the boxes I had spent the previous weeks packing. Within a few hours, the home we had occupied for 17 years was nearly empty. My husband watched me as I watched the movers, and he quietly asked, "Is this triggering you?"

I tilted my head to one side as I pondered his thoughtful question. When I was eight years old, my family moved from Arkansas to California. Everything we owned was loaded onto a U-Haul truck, and in the course of our cross-country move, the U-Haul truck was stolen. The police eventually found the perpetrators as they had just finished having a big yard sale—with our belongings!

Interviews with the neighbors later revealed that the same people who held the yard sale also had a large bonfire in their backyard the same night the U-Haul truck was stolen. Our birth certificates. Baby pictures. Family albums. Personal keepsakes. All of it. Burned. On purpose.

We had nothing left but the clothes on our backs and a second change of clothes in a suitcase in our old burgundy station wagon. After the theft and fire, we had to move in with my grandma while my family began the long process of rebuilding our lives.

Decades later, as my husband and I watched everything we own get loaded onto this new moving truck, I searched my heart for any residue of anxiety or fear over the possibility of it happening again. Would this truck get hijacked and robbed somewhere in the middle of the country? In my mind, I played out the scenario. What if it happened again? And then I knew. If it happened again, we'd be ok. I had total peace about it.

To my husband's question I replied, "No, I don't think so. This moving process has triggered some memories, but it hasn't triggered emotions. I can remember it without reliving it, and if it happened again and we had to replace all of our belongings, we could. It wouldn't be fun, but it wouldn't be the end of the world, either. I guess if anything good came out of what happened to my family all those years ago, it's that I don't get attached to stuff. There are only a few things in that truck I really care about. But they don't have monetary value; they have sentimental value. Like the blue-rose china tea set you gave me on our first anniversary. I would be sad to lose that."

My husband looked at me and said, "You know, we can put that box in the car with us."

I thought about it, too, for about a minute, and then said, "No, I don't want to do that. Perhaps this is an exercise in remembering what is truly important. I'll be ok if my tea set makes it, and I'll be ok if it doesn't."

None of us ever want to experience loss, but when—not if—we do, we can let the loss refine us and not define us.

When Loss Changes Us

We've all experienced loss in different ways. Perhaps you've lost everything you once owned to a hurricane or a house fire. Perhaps you've known the heartache of a lost dream—something you worked years for that never materialized. Perhaps you've experienced the loss of a job you enjoyed that allowed you to provide for your family. Perhaps you've lost your close-knit community because of a big move to another part of the country. Perhaps you've lost a part of your health, and you're navigating that tortuous road of trying to figure out a new normal. Or perhaps you've known the stinging loss of someone you loved.

Loss changes us. That part is inevitable. But we get to decide *how* it will change us. Will the hard circumstances we've endured change us for the better or the worse? None of us ever want to experience loss, but when—not if—we do, we can let the loss refine us and not define us.

Moses, the builder of God's sanctuary, was well-acquainted with loss. As a baby, he lost his family and his Hebrew heritage as he was adopted into an Egyptian household. As a prince of Pharaoh, he then lost the prestige of his position when he later fled Egypt as a fugitive. As a shepherd, he lost the ability to hide in obscurity when God called him to return to Egypt as a spokesman—a job he didn't want to do—for the Israelites. Then, as a leader of the Israelites, he eventually lost the privilege of entering the promised land due to his own sin.

Moses knew loss. But he also knew God. Personally. And that made all the difference, because God makes all the difference.

Paul, too, knew loss. The writer who instructs us to seek to lead a quiet life understood what it was like to live a "loud" life. He had a résumé that any good Jew could be proud of, but he left all that behind as he chose to follow Christ. Yet, he considered his losses to be his gain, because he gained Christ.

What if we considered our losses to be a gain? What if we looked on our sorrows as the entry point that God uses to enter into our lives in deeper ways? What if, through our losses, we come to understand how we truly gain a closer fellowship with Christ?

Part of cultivating a quiet heart means realizing that we have the power to choose how we respond to loss. This doesn't mean we will automatically respond to loss with a nonchalant shrug of our shoulders. There's a process for grieving, and it is important not to skip past that. But with time, as we invite the Holy Spirit to renew us from the inside out, our losses can be woven into a larger tapestry that becomes a beautiful story of redemption. This is what God does: he exchanges our ashes for his beauty (Isaiah 61:1-3).

A week after the moving truck was filled with our belongings, my husband and I stood on the front lawn of our new house on the opposite coast, and we watched as every piece of furniture and every single box was carried inside our new home. Everything made it just fine. And we gave thanks, knowing every gift is part of his grace.

TUNING IN TO QUIET

Contemplate

1. It's so easy to let our losses define us. In what ways have certain losses defined you in the past?
2. How can those same losses be redeemed as a way for God to refine you? In other words, how can your losses become entry points for God to enter into your life and for you to experience a closer fellowship with him?

3. How would you describe to someone who doesn't know Christ how you can consider your losses to be gain because of Christ?

Cultivate

So much of our earthly life is taken up with how others define us or how we define ourselves. The world especially loves to tell us that we ought to be the sole definer of our "true selves." But what if we let God define us and our losses refine us? I don't say this to minimize suffering. Not at all. But in God's hands, our suffering is given purpose. We may not always understand why some things happen as they do, but with God our suffering is placed within an eternal context. And a tearless eternity awaits. Today, let's be intentional about refusing to be defined by our losses. Instead, let's ask God to refine us by entering in through our losses to reveal more of himself to us.

Pray

Lord, thank you that we do not have to be defined by the losses we experience in this lifetime. As we yield to the furnace of affliction, our souls can be refined. Help us to hold loosely to the things of this earth and to keep our eyes fixed on you. For we will spend eternity with you, and the gift of your presence supersedes all else. In your kind name, Jesus, we pray. Amen.

Day 20

WHERE WE TURN WHEN LIFE TURNS HARD

"I am the vine; you are the branches. The one who remains in me and I in him produces much fruit, because you can do nothing without me."

John 15:5

When I turned 40, I wasn't thinking about the effects of aging. I wasn't thinking about the changes that naturally occur in a woman's 40-something body. And I wasn't thinking that it was the new 30 or anything like that. I was thinking about my cousin. We were close in age and had grown up together, yet he had died the year before of Ewing's Sarcoma, a rare but aggressive cancer. All I could think about on my 40th birthday was the fact that my cousin would never see his.

The last time I saw my cousin, he was struggling to find a comfortable position. The large tumor protruding from his back made it difficult for him to lie down. When the doctors removed it, the purpose was palliative: to help him lie in bed more comfortably. At home, he settled into the rhythms of hospice care, but there was a certain type of bandage for his back that he preferred. He showed me the box and asked if I would go to Walgreens to get him some more. I would have done anything if it had helped him feel more comfortable, so I gathered my keys and was starting for the door when he said, "'Nise, can I go with you?" He always called me 'Nise. And with that wry half-smile of his, he assured me, "I'll be all right. I just want to get outside a little bit."

He walked slowly with his robe wrapped around him loosely. After he had maneuvered his way into the front seat of the car, we used a couple of pillows to prop him up. When we pulled into the Walgreens parking lot, he waited in the car while I ran inside and bought all the boxes they had of that type of bandage. I showed him the bag full of bandages and asked, "How long will these last?"

"A few days," he said. "Thanks."

"Are you up for hitting another Walgreens?" I asked.

He nodded, so we took a drive to a few more Walgreens stores around the city, where I bought as many boxes of bandages as I could. On our way back to his house, he said, "You know, I live on Vine Street."

That much I knew, but he continued, "Before I got sick, I wasn't really following the Lord, but I've been praying a lot lately, and I think it's interesting that Jesus said he was the Vine, and in order for me to get home, you have to turn right up here on Ewing Street before you turn left onto Vine Street." He pointed to the upcoming intersection, and sure enough, the street sign said, "Ewing St." I turned right.

My cousin looked at the street sign as we turned the corner and said, "If it wasn't for this cancer, I wouldn't have turned back to Jesus. And just as you need to go down Ewing Street to reach Vine Street, I needed to go through Ewing's

I want you to know that whatever you've been through or whatever you are currently going through, you can get through it, and you will be ok on the other side of it.

Sarcoma in order to reach the true Vine, who is preparing my next home."

Not long after this, my cousin passed from this life to the next, where there is no cancer and no suffering. During his last days, my cousin experienced an unearthly peace—the kind that can only be found in Jesus—but I still had questions. I'm sure you've known someone, too, who suffered much too young and lost far too much.

A Soul Wrestling with God

Whenever life deals an unexpected blow and I am filled with questions, I turn to the obscure words of a minor prophet in the Old Testament. Habakkuk wrote a small portion of Scripture, just three chapters in total, and he doesn't get a lot of fanfare in churches today. He's lumped together with eleven other minor prophets. They're called "minor" because their contributions are rather short compared to the lengthier books by Isaiah, Jeremiah, Ezekiel, and Daniel. But the little book of Habakkuk is where I turn when life turns upside down.

Habakkuk was unlike other prophets. Where other prophets conveyed messages from God to his people, Habakkuk did the unexpected. Instead of declaring a message *from* God, he expressed his deepest concerns directly *to* God. Habakkuk didn't hold back, either. He wasn't afraid to ask the hard questions. His book reads like a deeply personal journal. He talked to God. Then God responded. Back and forth, a real dialogue ensued.

Habakkuk's posture was not one of haughty contempt; rather, his posture was one of honest bewilderment. I think a lot of us can relate. When something awful happens, the questions come pouring out of us. *Why did this have to happen? Where is God in all of this? Am I supposed to learn something here? If so, what?*

With bold words Habakkuk shows us that it's ok to come to God with our honest questions and sincere doubts. Fittingly, Habakkuk's name means "to wrestle" for that is exactly what he does in his writing. He wrestles with God, not literally like Jacob once did, but he wrestles with his pain through the words he writes. As a prophet, he foreknew that the Babylonians would attack Jerusalem, destroy the temple, and drive the Hebrews into exile. The Babylonians were known for their vicious warfare tactics, and the knowledge of this pending sorrow was almost too great for Habakkuk to bear. Why would God allow such a thing to happen to his people?

Writing through Our Grief

In one small way, I can identify with Habakkuk because I've always kept a journal, writing out my prayers and sharing the details of my day with God. I've never been one to hold back either, especially when it comes to the tempest of questions stirring in my heart.

You've likely had a few questions of your own, too. Questions about God and his goodness when your life feels like anything but good. If that's you, I want you to know you can open the pages of Scripture and then write to God in a journal exactly what you're feeling. It's ok to ask the hard questions and wrestle with the Bible's answers. Because I do believe the Bible has answers. More importantly, I believe the Bible points to the person who is the answer. He says that he is the vine and we are the branches.

Cultivating a quiet heart doesn't mean we move through our days with little or no reaction to the pain around us. It doesn't mean we don't feel the grief of sorrow upon sorrow.

But it does mean we know where to turn when life turns inside out.

I want you to know that whatever you've been through or whatever you are currently going through, you *can* get through it, and you *will* be ok on the other side of it. And you don't have to be alone for any of it. When life turns hard, we can assume the posture of Habakkuk and ask the hard questions. We can wrestle with what God wants to say to us through Scripture, and when all is said and done, we can know with deep assurance that Jesus is preparing a place for us. We may not always understand why some things happen as they do, but when we put our hope in the Vine, we experience a peace that defies all understanding.

TUNING IN TO QUIET

Contemplate

1. Where do you naturally turn when life turns hard?
2. Have you ever read the tiny book of Habakkuk? What does it say to you that God welcomed the sincere questions his prophet asked?
3. Do you feel comfortable going to God with your questions? Why or why not?

Cultivate

We all have questions. We can't help but wonder why God allows certain things to happen. Today, spend a few moments writing out your questions. It's ok to be real with God. He knows what is in our hearts anyway. Invite God into those places where there is confusion and doubt. Sit with him in those places. Let his word wash over you. Then thank him that he is the kind of God who welcomes the cries of his people, and he promises to listen to the cries of our hearts.

Pray

Lord, thank you that you have not left us alone to find our way through the tumultuous turns of life. You are with us when times are good, and you are with us when times are not. Thank you that we can come to you with our honest questions, and in your presence we find your comfort. Help us to look to you in every season, for in you alone we find everything we need. In your tender name, Jesus, we pray. Amen.

Day 21

EVEN ON THE FAR SIDE OF THE SEA

"Therefore say, 'This is what the Lord GOD says: Though I sent them far away among the nations and scattered them among the countries, yet for a little while I have been a sanctuary for them in the countries where they have gone.'"

Ezekiel 11:16

I've only had the opportunity to fly overseas one time. The lone stamp in my passport is from a small country in the Far East, a country that is closed to the gospel. I went as part of a team to teach English and converse with college students who desired to practice their English with native speakers. But in the days leading up to my departure, I felt apprehension. As much as I looked forward to the trip and felt certain I was called to go, doubt plagued me. Could something bad happen while I was there? My mind ran with narratives fit for a melodrama.

Does that ever happen to you, too? Do you ever worry about bad things that *might* happen? Or terrible things that *could* happen? Does your mind tend to lead you to worst-case scenarios? May heaven have mercy on us worriers!

I carried my apprehension with me every step through the airport, like an extra load of baggage no one could see. While

I tried to smile on the outside, I rehearsed on the inside a short passage from one of my favorite psalms:

> *Where can I go from your Spirit? Where can I flee from your presence? If I go up to the heavens, you are there; if I make my bed in the depths, you are there. If I rise on the wings of the dawn, if I settle on the far side of the sea, even there your hand will guide me, your right hand will hold me fast. (Psalm 139:7-10, NIV)*

Yes, even on the far side of the sea, God's hand would guide me and hold me. There is nowhere I can go, and nowhere you can go, where God cannot go, too.

I committed to memory those words from Psalm 139 as I embarked on a journey that took me farther than I had ever been, and I'm happy to report that nothing horrendous happened while I was overseas. But I was still glad to return to the soil of my homeland. Being in a country that did not openly embrace Christianity was a disquieting kind of experience. When the culture around you is averse to everything you believe to be true, it cements the reality that you're an alien in a foreign land.

That was over two decades ago. Nowadays, though, even here on the North American continent, our culture has grown increasingly hostile to the basic tenets of Christianity. More and more, we are living as exiles in our own Babylon of sorts. But through it all, God remains the sanctuary we need in any place and age.

A Different Kind of Sanctuary

When Solomon's temple replaced the tabernacle in the Old Testament, the newer sanctuary retained the same overall design as the tabernacle, except that it was lavishly adorned with even

God has promised to be our sanctuary, whether we're on the far side of the sea or at home in our living rooms.

more gold and jewels. But the majesty of this temple could not contain God, for he consistently maintained that he would not dwell forever among an idolatrous people. After many generations of exceeding patience, God finally removed himself from the midst of his rebellious people and left the temple. The Babylonians then attacked Jerusalem—pillaging the city, leveling the temple, and carrying a remnant of Hebrews into exile (2 Kings 25:1-11).

And yet, even there in Babylon, when all hope seemed forever lost, God spoke through the prophet Ezekiel these tender words of hope:

> *Therefore say, "This is what the Lord GOD says: Though I sent them far away among the nations and scattered them among the countries, yet for a little while I have been a sanctuary for them in the countries where they have gone".*
>
> *(Ezekiel 11:16)*

Even when God's people experienced the Lord's discipline for their repeated sin, God promised to be a sanctuary for them. It wouldn't be the kind of sanctuary they were used to, with the Shekinah[13] glory of the tabernacle or the rich magnificence of the temple, but God would become a sanctuary for them, right where they were, even as they lived in exile.

As horrific as the Babylonian invasion was, there was grace in the fact that God used this moment in time to help his people understand that he is not confined to a single space. God could be with them wherever they went, even in a place like Babylon. The same can be true of us, in whichever place we call home.

It is good to look forward to that day when we shall see God face to face, but until that glorious day, God has promised to be our sanctuary, whether we're on the far side of the sea or at home in our living rooms.

My early dreams of travelling around the world never materialized beyond that one brief visit to a foreign land. For the most part, my life has settled into an everyday kind of ordinary. Raising three kids. Driving a gray minivan. And doing household chores—all while trying to figure out a more interesting way to cook chicken. But even as I go about my mostly ordinary days, my heart is freed from the noise around me because I know God is my sanctuary, wherever I go.

TUNING IN TO QUIET

Contemplate

1. Have you ever traveled to a distant country? If so, what was it like? If not, is there somewhere you would like to go someday?
2. How do the words of Psalm 139 bring comfort to you, knowing that God is with you wherever you go, whether you're in your living room or on the far side of the sea?
3. Are you used to thinking of a sanctuary as a literal place? How does your view of the idea of sanctuary change knowing that God is your sanctuary, even in the midst of ordinary days?

Cultivate

Think of all the places you go to as a normal part of your week. Your house. Target. The grocery store. Target. The Post Office. Target. Ok, I'm kidding about Target (sort of). But seriously, as you think of the places you go to every week, picture God there with you. Because he really is. Then give thanks. Thank him for being with you in your car. Thank him for being with you at the doctor's office. Thank him for being with you at the dry cleaners. For he is with you. Everywhere. There is nowhere you can go where he cannot go, too.

Pray

Lord, thank you for being the sanctuary we need from a world that screams with messages that are counter to your ways. Even as we live as exiles in a land that rejects you, we are never without your calming presence and your comforting embrace. You are the sweet refuge we can turn to, for you are with us always. We love you and praise you. In your precious name, Jesus, we pray. Amen.

Day 22

THE HABIT OF GATHERING

"And let us consider one another in order to provoke love and good works, not neglecting to gather together, as some are in the habit of doing, but encouraging each other, and all the more as you see the day approaching."

Hebrews 10:24-25

I didn't realize how much I missed church. Where we lived, almost a year of Covid lockdowns meant "online church," but when the doors opened again, we were there.

I love church. Despite its many flaws and deep brokenness, I can't stay away, partly because I know I bring my own flaws and brokenness with me. I appreciate the rhythm of showing up every week, whether I feel like it or not, because I know once I get there, I will be glad. I enjoy the general hum of people chatting in the courtyard, and I love getting to hug my Tuesday-evening Bible-study friends from every generation.

But my favorite part of every Sunday morning service is that quiet moment when we partake in communion. More than a tiny morsel of bread and a thimble-sized cup from the vine, communion is that moment in the service when everything goes soft and still. That moment when you can lower your head and remember the cross and thank Jesus for the sacrifice he made. That moment when you can confess your trespasses and ask God for his forgiveness. That moment when you can intercede for your family's most pressing needs.

While I know that God is with me everywhere I go, even on the far side of the sea, I also know that he has adopted every believer into his family, and it's important that we gather with his family regularly. It's part of God's design for his people.

While I utilize digital technology every day, I'll always maintain that real-life relationships surpass online connections, which is why it's important that we gather with other flesh-and-blood humans to sing of God's goodness and hear the word preached. We weren't meant to live in isolation. We were designed by our Creator to live in community.

In his book called *Analog Church*, Pastor Jay Kim writes:

> *The digital age has amplified our ability to communicate at the tragic cost of our aptitude for communing ...*
> *To communicate is primarily about the exchange of information. To commune is primarily about the exchange of presence. To be sure, communicating isn't always simple and it isn't always easy. Miscommunication happens all the time. But to commune is the more difficult task. It requires more of us: more of our attention, empathy, and compassion. In light of this, why must community within the context of the church be analog? Because while we can certainly communicate digitally, we can only commune in analog.*[14]

We can only commune in analog. In real space and time. Where we can touch and hold one another. Where we can lean in and listen to one another.

We communicate our care for one another when we're actually there for one another.

The church is God's gift to the world. As broken as it sometimes can be, the church is still God's chosen vessel for reaching people, and we communicate our care for one another when we're actually there for one another. To talk, laugh, cry, listen, and share a meal together. Even in that old tent-sanctuary, the idea of fellowshipping in God's presence and eating a meal together held eminent importance.

The Bread of Presence

As mentioned earlier, the gold lampstand lit the Holy Place, but across from that lampstand was a gold table with twelve loaves of bread (Exodus 25:23-30). These twelve loaves were called the "bread of presence" because they represented the twelve tribes of Israel and they were placed in God's presence inside the sanctuary.[15] This symbolically demonstrated that God was in the midst of his people.

Every Sabbath the priests would replace the twelve loaves with freshly baked ones. The priests would then eat the older loaves right there in the Holy Place (Leviticus 24:5-9). They literally broke bread and ate it inside the sanctuary in God's presence. To share a meal with someone is to fellowship with them; in the same way, the priests "fellowshipped" with God as they ate bread in the sanctuary.[16]

God desires the same fellowship with us today.

While a version of online church will likely continue as an option—and it may be a wise option for those who are homebound or immunocompromised—we can't forget what the church was designed to be. A place where people can gather to sing praises to God. A place where people can hear the word proclaimed with boldness. And a place where people can taste the bread and sip the cup and remember how good God is.

As we continue this journey toward cultivating a quiet heart, it's of paramount importance that we are part of a local church body. God is with you wherever you go, but he also has something special to give you through his body, his family. If you're hesitant, I understand. It's not always easy, I know. There are hurts and disappointments aplenty, but when we show up with our own broken selves and offer worship to the one true God, something happens. God is blessed, and so are we.

TUNING IN TO QUIET

Contemplate

1. What is your favorite part of attending church? Who would you miss the most if you were not there?
2. It's easy to list all the things that are "wrong" with the church today, whether we're talking about the global church or the local church down the street from our house. But what are some of the things that are right? Make a list of all the ways in which your local church is a blessing.
3. Why is it only possible to commune in real space and time?

Cultivate

Communion is more than the bread and the cup. It means to commune with God among his people. Those people aren't perfect. Not by a long shot. But neither are we. One of the reasons why I can confidently step through the doors of a church building today is the fact that I know my own brokenness, and I know I'm going to find broken people on the other side of those doors, too. I'm supposed to. Because our brokenness is being made whole at the foot of the cross. And we can experience healing together. Today, consider your habit of attendance. For most people in North America, attendance has become hit-and-miss for a lot of reasons. But whatever your pattern has been—whether ultra-regular or inconsistent at best—embrace the habit of gathering regularly with God's people.

Pray

Lord, thank you that you not only call us your own, but you have brought us into your family. Forgive us when we are tempted to go it alone. Remind us that we were created to fellowship in your presence. We are so grateful for the family you have surrounded us with. May we be active participants in loving others through our local church body. In your sweet name, Jesus, we pray. Amen.

Day 23

THE POWER OF SILENCE

"In the same way the Spirit also helps us in our weakness, because we do not know what to pray for as we should, but the Spirit himself intercedes for us with inexpressible groanings."

Romans 8:26

As I lay in a hospital bed struggling to breathe, I couldn't pray much of anything beyond "God, please help." My words were more desperate than eloquent, but they were real. And that's what God is looking for. Not fancy-schmancy prayers. But pleas from the depths of our being. Sometimes that's all we have to give. Thankfully, it's enough.

Our prayers don't have to be lengthy, verbose offerings. Simple utterances can suffice, for our words can be the equivalent of the widow's two mites when offered with a sincere heart. That's what I experienced when my impaired lungs struggled to squeeze out audible words. Even if I tried to pray silently inside my heart, the pain proved too distracting. My groanings were more exact. Which is why I'm so grateful that God understands even these and provides for us in those moments when we don't know what to say or how to pray.

Paul says, "The Spirit … helps us in our weakness." This could mean physical weakness, but it could also imply spiritual weakness. When we're distraught beyond words and we don't know how to pray, "the Spirit himself intercedes for us with inexpressible groanings" (Romans 8:26). What a gift this is to God's people. When we fall short, which is often, God always comes through.

Have you experienced a season when you just didn't know how to pray? When you weren't even sure what to pray for? All you knew was that you needed help. Real help. In a big way. And only God in heaven could understand the depth of your pain. I've been there, too. It's never fun, but God has consistently shown himself faithful. Every time.

Prayer is indispensable when our world is falling apart, and it's all we've got left. But it's also indispensable when life is rolling along pretty well. We just usually have a harder time seeing the necessity of prayer when times are good.

Daily Dependence on God

I've never considered myself much of a prayer warrior. Even when I am healthy and strong, I don't exactly experience fire from heaven when I pray. Sometimes my prayers feel flat and not like the vibrant word-offerings I sometimes hear from others. But prayer is still a central part of every believer's life, for it's a fundamental way in which we express our dependence on God. When we go to him daily with our thanks and our needs, we express our acknowledgment that we cannot supply anything for ourselves. We look to God for everything we need.

This is why, when Jesus taught his disciples to pray, he didn't say that we should pray for our *weekly bread* or our *monthly bread* or *enough bread to last us a year*. Jesus instructed

This idea of daily dependence on God is counter to everything we hear in the world, but it's an elemental part in cultivating a quiet life.

his followers to pray for their "daily bread" (Matthew 6:11). Just as the manna once fell daily from heaven, when we pray for our daily bread, we express our daily dependence on God as our provider and sustainer, for he holds the power over every aspect of the universe.

This idea of daily dependence on God is counter to everything we hear in the world, but it's an elemental part in cultivating a quiet life. When we're convinced that God will provide what we need, we don't have to stress or worry. We are free to live each day with open hands to receive whatever the Father has for us that day.

Maybe for you prayer is a vital part of your everyday life. Or maybe prayer is something you know you're supposed to do, but you're not always sure how. If you're not sure where to start, I want to encourage you to begin with silence. I know we're focusing mostly on a quiet life stemming from an inner quietness of heart, and that's what it is, but it's also wise to experience actual quiet from time to time, too. And whenever we're not sure how to pray, we can lean into the silence and let the Spirit do his work in us.

Experiencing Deep Quiet

To experience deep quiet, take an inventory of the sounds around you. Then turn off as many sounds as possible. The radio, the television, and the notifications on your phone. If possible, try to designate a period of time when the dishwasher, washing machine, and dryer are not running. If you're able to combine your silence with solitude, then you're likely to have fewer interruptions, but if you have family members in your house, give everyone a heads-up that you're going to spend a few minutes in quiet. That way they know not to knock on your door for a little bit. Set a specified time, too. Maybe begin with 15 to 30 minutes—whatever you feel most comfortable with.

For some of us, we may be so unaccustomed to actual silence that we find it eerie or unsettling at first. Such times of quiet have become so foreign in our culture that we almost don't know what to do with ourselves when we experience a moment of silence. If that's you, it's okay. Perhaps shorten the amount of time to begin with, but do commit to it periodically. You'll be surprised at how beneficial it is for the soul.

Let the power of silence be the birthplace of a renewed prayer life. For when we are still, God does his best work.

TUNING IN TO QUIET

Contemplate

1. Have you experienced a season when you just didn't know how to pray? When words evaded you? How would you describe such a season to someone else?
2. How does prayer signify our dependence on God?
3. Do you ever intentionally turn off all the sounds around you? Why or why not?

Cultivate

Once you've settled in for a few minutes of silence and solitude, avoid the urge to fill the silence. Let the quiet wash over you. Then try reading the psalms, for they give us words when we don't have many ourselves. Then praise God and tell him what you're grateful for. It's often said that gratitude is the cure for spiritual amnesia, and I don't think that's very far off the mark. Then share with God what your most pressing needs are. Finally, spend some time praying for others. Then thank God for being a God who hears us when we pray. Growing a prayer life is vital for anyone seeking to cultivate a quiet heart, but it likely won't happen overnight for any of us. Prayer takes time. But God is patient. He is good like that.

Pray

Lord, thank you that we can come to you with prayers that might sound unimpressive to human ears, but you receive our prayers when we offer them with sincere hearts. Help us to embrace times of silence and solitude as a discipline for listening to you through your word, and remind us, Lord, that we are dependent upon you for everything. We praise you for being our faithful provider. In your gracious name, Jesus, we pray. Amen.

Day 24

WHERE OUR FOCUS LIES

"He must increase, but I must decrease."

John 3:30

As I sat with a new group of friends, I listened as each person introduced themselves with a combination of capital letters and numbers. One person said, "I'm an ESFJ and a 9." Everyone nodded in comprehension. Another person said, "I'm an INFP, an HSP, and a 6." Again, everyone nodded.

The popularity of personality typing cannot be overstated. It's become a shorthand way of introducing ourselves. Thus, given the prevalence of personality typing today, we might mistakenly think that a quiet life is synonymous with introversion or one of the quieter temperaments. But leading a quiet life has nothing to do with being an introvert or an extrovert, being reserved or talkative.

If we look to Paul, who admonished believers to lead a quiet life, we see that Paul wasn't exactly "the quiet type." He was bold and decisive and never afraid to speak his mind in public venues, even if it meant being flogged! So, cultivating a quiet life isn't just for the quieter folks among us. It's for all of us because it's not about our personality or our temperament.

It's about the state of our hearts, and the state of our hearts is dependent upon the focus of our hearts.

A Different Kind of Motto

Our culture implores us to focus intensely on ourselves, but this actually leads to a restless heart; whereas, when our focus is on Christ in all we say and do, our hearts are at rest. This is why some of the most vocal and outspoken people in the Bible can be said to have lived quiet lives. Their focus wasn't on themselves; it was on Christ.

Take John the Baptist, for example. He was described as a voice calling in the wilderness, and he preached a loud message of repentance (Mark 1:2-4). But John's whole mission was to point others to something greater than himself. Indeed, he pointed everyone to the Messiah, even to the point of diminishing his own following (John 3:26). While he loudly proclaimed the truth, John the Baptist possessed a quiet heart because the desire of his heart was simply this: "He must increase, but I must decrease" (v 30). This was his motto, and it's the essence of a quiet heart. It's a heart that finds genuine contentment in pointing others to something—to Someone!—greater than oneself.

This is also why the digital realm is such a noisy place. It's populated with many hearts whose motto is "I must increase!" which is the opposite of John's heart. But as we aim to cultivate a quiet life, this can be our motto: *More of Jesus. Less of me.* Which will mean… *More Scripture. Less social media. More prayer. Less podcasts. More godly books. Less blogs. More time with you. Less with YouTube.*

It's not that social media and podcasts are bad. It's not that blogs and YouTube videos are bad, either. We can enjoy all of those things… to a degree. It's more about where we primarily

The sanctuary was a place of true peace because it pointed to Christ, and only in Christ do we find genuine peace.

devote our time and our focus, because the things we give our attention to are the things that shape and mold us.

Our desire is to be shaped and formed by Scripture. We want to be attuned to the right things through prayer. We want to be involved in our local church. We want to hear the voices of age and experience through old books and new. And when space and distance allow, we want to spend time, one on one, face to face, with real-life friends.

To be sure, cultivating a quiet life isn't about removing ourselves from social media entirely or rejecting all things digital; rather, it's about making sure the digital world doesn't take over our lives. It's also an honest recognition that the call to lead a quiet life is not likely to draw a large crowd. Just the opposite, in fact. In the world's eyes, a quiet life might seem unimpressive because its values are so different from the world's values. The quiet life is a gentle embrace of the unassuming dailyness of life, and it's the way of peace.

We do all of these things because we want our lives to point to something greater than ourselves. We want our lives to point to Christ.

Pointing to Christ

Everything about the tabernacle/temple sanctuary pointed to Christ. The altar, where daily sacrifices took place, pointed to the ultimate once-and-for-all sacrifice that Christ would make on the cross. The bronze basin by the entrance typified the cleansing that is necessary before we enter God's presence. The gold lamp inside the Holy Place pointed God's people to Christ as the Light of the world. The bread of presence on the gold table showed them that God dwelled among his people and wanted to fellowship with them. And the veil showed that it would be only through Christ's sacrifice that we would be granted access to the heavenly Most Holy Place in his presence.

The sanctuary was a place of true peace because it pointed to Christ, and only in Christ do we find genuine peace.

Maybe this idea of cultivating a quiet life sounds exactly like what you've been desiring for a long time. Or maybe you feel like you're automatically disqualified from leading a quiet life because you have a naturally vivacious and outgoing personality. Maybe you were the nonstop talker in class, and the teacher always had to ask you to be quiet. That's ok! Whether you feel you are more prone to being chatty or more drawn to being reserved, the quiet life is for everybody because it has to do with the focus of our hearts and not with how we might rate ourselves on the scale of talkativeness.

And all God's extroverts said, "Amen!"

TUNING IN TO QUIET

Contemplate

1. How would you rate yourself on a scale of talkativeness? Do you consider yourself more of an introvert or extrovert?
2. How would you explain to an extrovert that leading a quiet life has nothing to do with one's natural temperament?
3. What kinds of online activities attract large followings? Why is a quiet life not really conducive to attracting large followings?

Cultivate

The world of social media is oftentimes likened to an economy of attention. Those with the largest followings are those who attract the most attention. This then encourages social-media users to do whatever they can to garner more and more attention. It's no wonder the online world is so loud. This is the opposite of John the Baptist's focus; he genuinely wanted to decrease the amount of attention on himself so more attention could be on Christ. Since our focus follows our attention, spend a day following your focus. Today, in both your online spaces and your real-life places, note the conversations you have, the posts you read, and the stories you hear about. How often are these conversations, posts, and stories pointing you to Christ? Or, how often are they pointing you to the person who is sharing? Then begin to be more selective in where you direct your focus.

Pray

Lord, thank you for the beautiful diversity we find in your creation. In your manifold wisdom, you created each of us to be unique, and you are glorified by the work of your hands. When we are tempted to focus on ourselves, help us to retrain our focus on you. Help us to lead lives that point others to the greatness of who you are, for your ways are higher than our ways, and your thoughts are higher than our thoughts. And we desire to decrease so that you may increase. We worship you, Lord, with all adoration. In your magnificent name, Jesus, we pray. Amen.

Day 25

VESSELS OF PURPOSE

"God has chosen what is foolish in the world to shame the wise, and God has chosen what is weak in the world to shame the strong."

1 Corinthians 1:27

One Saturday morning I gathered with my Tuesday-night gals. Normally, we met on Tuesday evenings to prepare the fellowship hall for our women's Bible study; we'd spread out the tablecloths, set out the centerpieces, and arrange a buffet of food. One sweet lady in particular would always show up early to make two large cannisters of coffee: one regular, one decaf. But on this frosty Saturday morning, we wanted to show up for her because she was sitting on the front pew of the sanctuary, preparing to say goodbye to her husband.

As the memorial service began, I looked down my row at the women sitting next to each other. All of them were from our Tuesday-evening Bible study, and almost all of them, I noticed, were also widows. They sat together in such solidarity because they knew what it was like to sit on the front row. They knew.

While the world outside carried on as normal, my world that morning changed as I witnessed a beautiful ministry taking place. These women didn't have an official title on the church's staff. They didn't receive any remuneration from the church's payroll. But their ministry was palpable. Their presence felt.

All these years later, I can't remember a single sermon I ever heard in that sanctuary, even though I attended every Sunday morning service. But I will forever remember the message I received as I watched these beautiful women gather to support their sister as her life radically shifted.

A Soul Never Goes Unnoticed

In biblical times, widows were often the poorest of the poor. Relegated to the margins of society, they were overlooked and sometimes forgotten. And yet, not one soul ever goes unnoticed by God, and oftentimes he chooses those who are considered "lowly" in the eyes of the world to minister to others in significant ways. This was the case with Elijah, a prophet on the run from Israel's King Ahab and Queen Jezebel, who were doing their level best to murder all of God's prophets. God told Elijah to go to a widow's house in Zarephath, which happened to be in enemy territory.

Due to a severe famine, people everywhere were starving, so it wasn't exactly convenient for this widow to have a fugitive show up at her house asking for bread. She told him plainly that she had just enough oil and flour left for one last meal—for herself and her son—and then she expected to die.

> *Then Elijah said to her, "Don't be afraid; go and do as you have said. But first make me a small loaf from it and bring it out to me. Afterward, you may make some for yourself and your son, for this is what the LORD God of Israel says, 'The flour jar will not become empty and the oil jug*

On our own, we may not feel like we have much to offer, but with God, all things are possible.

> *will not run dry until the day the LORD sends rain on the surface of the land.'" So she proceeded to do according to the word of Elijah. (1 Kings 17:13-15)*

And just like that, she went and did as Elijah said? Now I don't know about you, but if all I've got left is enough flour and oil to make one last meal for my only child and myself, I'm not sure I would just go and do as Elijah said. I might have said, "Sorry, buddy, you're on your own."

But the widow of Zarephath was obedient to what the prophet asked of her, and then, just as Elijah said, the jar of flour did not become empty, and the jug of oil did not run dry. A miracle of multiplication happened, where the flour just kept coming, and the oil just kept pouring.

Vessels of Purpose

There wasn't anything special about those vessels of flour and oil. They were ordinary household containers, much like the everyday cannisters that sit atop our kitchen counters holding flour and sugar. But God chose to use those ordinary vessels for a miraculous purpose, and the lives of the woman, her son, and the prophet Elijah were saved.

Similarly, every person is a vessel, too. We're vessels of flesh and bone. On our own, we may not feel like we have much to offer, but with God, all things are possible. As believers, we have the Holy Spirit living inside us, so we are walking vessels of his truth and goodness. And as we pour truth and goodness into the lives of others, we are pointing to something greater.

The widow of Zarephath probably didn't realize just how much her life was pointing to something greater. While the miracle of the unending flour and oil is cool, something else was happening here, too. Hundreds of years later, when Jesus steps into a synagogue at the beginning of his earthly ministry, he reads from the scroll of Isaiah and announces that he is the Messiah that Isaiah prophesied about. Then he tells the story of Elijah and the widow of Zarephath.

> *He also said, "Truly I tell you, no prophet is accepted in his hometown. But I say to you, there were certainly many widows in Israel in Elijah's days, when the sky was shut up for three years and six months while a great famine came over all the land. Yet Elijah was not sent to any of them except a widow at Zarephath in Sidon." (Luke 4:24-26)*

Through this widow's story, Christ declares himself to be the Giver of Life—the one who can provide for the needs of his children and the one who can defeat death. Not only that, but the fact that this widow was not an Israelite is significant, for this is one of the earliest indicators in Scripture that God's grace would extend not only to Jews but to all people. And her obedience is remembered and retold by Jesus himself.

The widow of Zarephath likely didn't know the extent to which her life pointed to something—and Someone!—far greater. She was simply being obedient to the task in front of her. She sacrificed what she had to make bread for someone in need.

In a similar way, the same can be said of us today. We may not ever know in this life the extent to which the Lord will use our circumstances to point others to him. Our task is to be faithful to do what is in front of us. The task before us may not seem all that important, but as we quietly go about the work before us, God is working in ways we cannot see. This is what it means to lead a quiet life. And this is what I witnessed in the sanctuary that morning when I attended a memorial service for an older friend. I saw women who gathered, who held hands, who prayed, and who comforted.

Wherever you are today, you can be like the women I witnessed. Even if our circumstances are different, we can still be women who show up for one another. We can be vessels of hope and encouragement, and we can trust that as we serve others, our lives are pointing to something greater.

TUNING IN TO QUIET

Contemplate

1. Why does God consistently choose what is lowly in the eyes of the world to do great things for his kingdom?
2. How might this truth give you hope as you pursue a quiet life?
3. Who do you know who has lived a full life and has stayed true to following God to their very last days? How has this person exhibited a life that focuses on Christ and on serving others?

Cultivate

The people who go the distance—the ones who stay faithful in their walk with God to their very last days—are usually people who remain intently focused on Christ and on serving others, and not on themselves. Do you have someone like this in your life? No matter how old we may be, we are never too old to look to someone whose life we would like to emulate. Who is that person in your life? If you don't have someone like that in your life, begin looking around on Sunday morning. Find an older saint whose footsteps you can follow. Ask them if they'd like to meet for coffee. Do what you can to spend time with someone older than you who can model for you what it looks like to have God increase while they decrease.

Pray

Lord, thank you that we are never alone in our grief, for you send your servants to gather around us and to comfort us with their presence. Help us to remember that, as we trust you and serve others, you are using our lives to point to you in ways we may never fully know on this side of eternity. But we trust you are working all things together for the good of those who love you, even when we can't fully understand what that looks like right now. We give you all the praise and glory. In your majestic name, Jesus, we pray. Amen.

Day 26

FROM THE OVERFLOW

"For the mouth speaks from the overflow of the heart."

Matthew 12:34

In the very back of the store, I found what I was looking for. Four alarm clocks. Remember those? They don't fit in your back pocket. They don't wrap around your wrist. They don't do your math homework for you. And they don't allow you to talk to people on the other side of the world. They simply plug into the wall and ring when you tell them to. It's the way a lot of us grew up waking up. Nowadays, though, it's common to have a smartphone on the nightstand next to our bed.

The young cashier squinted at my purchases, as if to say, "You know nobody uses these anymore, right?" Yeah, I know. But I had declared every bedroom in my home a phone-free zone. Again. I'm pretty sure I had done this before. But you know how you can dust a room one week, and a week later the same room needs dusting again? I think family phone rules are the same. You can state the boundaries one week, and maybe a week or a year later, they might need restating.

I have no idea what happened to our old alarm clocks. Somehow they vanished as the cooler, more convenient "alarm clocks" replaced them. So, it was time to reestablish the phone boundaries in our house. Simply put, no phones in bedrooms. Bedrooms are for sleeping and changing clothes and other things. And those are private things. No phones necessary. The phones can charge overnight on the kitchen counter.

Whole books are now being written on how to live "tech-wise" and "tech-healthy," and these are important conversations to have. We need more phone-free zones in our lives, where people can turn off the pinging and be with the people they love. I am convinced that certain phone boundaries are necessary for the sake of our overall health. At the same time, regular "life hacks" are not the ultimate answer. Things like periodic breaks from social media and phone-free zones in the house are very wise practices for a lot of reasons, but ultimately, the aim of this book is less about life hacks and more about entering God's presence and experiencing his peace as we cultivate a quiet heart in a noisy and demanding world.

Since going the way of the Luddites isn't exactly a realistic option for most of us, we have to figure out a way to incorporate digital technology into our daily lives without it taking over our lives. And the answer isn't found in life hacks but in this: when our digital interactions stem from the overflow of richly cultivated lives that are deeply rooted in the real world, then our participation online reflects greater health and integrity.

In other words, we should prioritize the local-tangible over the global-digital. When we are deeply committed to local relationships and tangible activities, our online involvement remains tethered to the real world. Thus, our global and

The health of our digital interactions will directly correlate with the health of our real-life commitments.

digital participation comes from the overflow of our local and tangible lives. Real people and real activities come first. When we have this rightly ordered in our lives, our online interactions become a reflection of genuine health.

The Overflow Principle

Jesus explained the overflow principle when he said, "For the mouth speaks from the overflow of the heart" (Matthew 12:34). Whatever is in our hearts will eventually come out through our mouths. Thus, what is invisible on the inside will be made visible on the outside. It's only a matter of time. To illustrate this, Jesus gave the example of a fruit tree. A good tree will produce good fruit, and a bad tree will produce bad fruit. Again, what is on the inside will be made known on the outside.

This same overflow principle applies to our online lives. The health of our digital interactions will directly correlate with the health of our real-life commitments. When we are committed to growing strong relationships with the people we live with and work with and go to church with, then from that wellspring of relational life we are able to give to others in a digital context. When this gets backward—when a person invests themselves first and foremost in an online format—then dysfunction ensues.

In my house, I still believe it's wise to keep smartphones out of bedrooms, but more than anything, I want to place a greater focus on the importance of investing in real relationships and tangible activities. So, when I do share something online, you can trust that it's from the overflow of a rich and beautiful life: one that is deeply connected with the humans I live and work with.

TUNING IN TO QUIET

Contemplate

1. What are some of your favorite life hacks for establishing healthy boundaries with your smartphone?
2. Why do you think Jesus chose the example of the fruit tree to illustrate the overflow principle?
3. Where have you observed the overflow principle at work (whether at work or school or church)?

Cultivate

We oftentimes think of our priorities as a top-down list, but today I'd like for us to think of our priorities as a series of concentric circles. On a piece of paper or in your journal, draw a circle and then draw four more circles around it. Write "God" in the very center circle to reflect the truth that God is the center of your life. In the next circle, write the names of the people you are closest to in real life, most likely your family members. Then in the next circle, write the names of those you interact with the most on a daily basis: your friends and neighbors and coworkers. Then write the names of people you fellowship with on a weekly basis at church. (There's likely to be some overlap here.) Lastly, write the names of people you interact with far and wide. This could be through any social-media means. As you move forward in cultivating a quiet life, remember that your life will flow from the center outward. A healthy relationship with God will overflow into a healthier relationship with your family, then your friends, and so forth.

Pray

Lord, thank you for creating a world that testifies to your goodness and beauty. When we are tempted to withdraw from the good world you have made and retreat to an intangible manmade world, draw us back to you and the world you spoke into existence. Help us to prioritize the places we find ourselves in and the people we find ourselves with. In this way, may the words we share digitally pour from the overflow of the lives we live tangibly. In your loving name, Jesus, we pray. Amen.

Day 27

A SWEET RESPITE FOR THE SOUL

"The heavens declare the glory of God, and the expanse proclaims the work of his hands."

Psalm 19:1

Working from home was awesome. At first. My schedule was flexible. I had no commute. I could take on the projects I truly loved. And best of all, I could wear comfy clothes all day, except for when I needed to be on a Zoom call, but even then I could still wear pajama pants and no one would ever know. Yes, there were definitely some benefits to working from home. But it came with a downside, too.

The separation between work and home blurred. Without a way to physically leave my work every day, I lived and breathed my work. Far too often I stayed up hours past everyone else's bedtime just to get a little more work done. Worse still, when you work all day on a computer, you become very sedentary, which isn't good for your physical health. Worst of all, I noticed the way my interactions were mostly with people who didn't live in my time zone, much less my zip code. Thanks to the convenience of modern technology, all my interactions were with people who lived thousands of miles away. Meanwhile, my relationships where I lived atrophied. Something needed to give.

I don't think working from home was the real problem, though. The real problem was the fact that I was overly invested in online interactions, both professionally and personally, because—let's face it—we oftentimes become friends with those we work with. So, more and more, I was investing in relationships with people who lived very far from me. And this is to say nothing of the fact that such a sedentary lifestyle wasn't working for me. I needed to move more. I needed to get outside. I needed fresh air. For my body and my soul.

Maybe you work from home, too, and you can relate. Or maybe you don't work from home, but you do work in front of a computer all day. Or maybe in your off-hours, you've noticed that you spend more time chatting online with people who don't live nearby than with the people you actually see in person throughout the week. Or maybe your temptation is Netflix or Amazon Prime or Apple TV or Hulu or one of the many other streaming options; maybe you've succumbed to the sedentary nature of binge-watching a few too many shows every day. If you can relate to any of the above, you're not alone.

One of the most subtly pernicious effects of modern technology is the way it seduces us into a sedentary lifestyle devoid of much human interaction. In the last chapter we discussed the importance of investing in local and tangible relationships and activities as this is paramount to our health. At the same time, it's also crucial that we recognize the way technology woos us into indoor isolation. We can easily spend hours upon hours in front of a screen. But there's a better way

There's something about entering into the beauty of God's created world that reorients our souls to what is real and what really matters.

to live. One of the best decisions I ever made was to physically walk away from my computer and go outside. Every day.

A Different Kind of Sanctuary

I found a park close to my house with a paved path around the perimeter, and I started going for daily walks. This little park has become something of a sanctuary: a place free of computers where my mind is free to take in my surroundings. The jacarandas and liquidambars line the path while tall oaks provide cool shade. Round and round I walk the circle—sometimes with worship music playing in my earbuds, and other times with nothing but the whisper of the wind ushering a sweet silence, inviting the soul to linger and listen.

Most mornings you can find me walking my favorite path. I start early, before the sun shows her full glory, because I like shade, and I love the quiet calm of a waking day. It's still a relatively new habit. Going on three years now. But what began as some basic exercise—and an intentional step away from my computer—became something more, something deeper. Now I can hardly start the day any other way.

In addition to my favorite local park, I also happen to be a big fan of national parks like Yosemite and Yellowstone, the Grand Canyon and the Grand Tetons. But we don't need the majesty of a grand scene to savor a brief respite of stillness and beauty. We can be intentional about setting aside a few moments each day, right where we are, to embrace the slow and savor the quiet.

There's something about entering into the beauty of God's created world that reorients our souls to what is real and what really matters. Something as simple as strolling through a park can anchor us in ways that scrolling on a screen cannot. It doesn't surprise me that the very first sanctuary was a garden, with rivers and trees and flowers and hills and rocks and birds and every kind of animal. The psalmist exclaims, "The heavens declare the glory of God, and the expanse proclaims the world of his hands" (Psalm 19:1). The heavens. The sky. The clouds. The stars. All of it declares God's glory. As does the earth. All of creation sings his praise, and we join in that chorus of praise when we step outside to behold his majesty with awe and wonder.

Friends, one of the easiest ways to cultivate a quiet heart in a noisy and demanding world is to close the laptop, turn off the TV, and power down the phone; then step outside to marvel at the beauty of all that God has made.

TUNING IN TO QUIET

Contemplate

1. Have you ever visited a national park? If so, which one? If not, which one most interests you and why?
2. What is one way you actively seek to combat the sedentary nature of using technology?
3. In your own words, how would you explain to someone that being outside in God's creation is like being in his sanctuary?

Cultivate

On Day 6, I encouraged you to step outside and enjoy the beauty of a sunset or sunrise. Today I'm going to encourage you to do something similar, yet different. Find a place outside that is especially beautiful to you. Maybe it's your favorite spot at the beach, if you happen to live near an ocean or lake. Or maybe it's a shady spot in your backyard, next to some lovely hydrangeas. Or maybe it's a local park, with tall trees and winding paths. Select someplace outdoors that is easy to get to from your house and make it your "sanctuary" where you can regularly savor the beauty of God's creation. Set aside time, regularly, to be in God's presence, in the sanctuary of his amazing creation without the noisy distractions of modern technology.

Pray

Thank you, Lord, for revealing something of the beautiful nature of who you are through the beauty of your creation. Thank you that we can be near you in the sanctuary of your own making. Whether we're in the lowest valley or on the highest mountain peak, we are never alone, for you are with us always. When the noise of this world reaches deafening levels, remind us that we can find a sweet respite for our souls in your presence, for you lead us beside quiet waters. In your sweet name, Jesus, we pray. Amen.

Day 28

A LIFE POURED OUT

"As they were eating, Jesus took bread, blessed and broke it, gave it to the disciples, and said, 'Take and eat it; this is my body.' Then he took a cup, and after giving thanks, he gave it to them and said, 'Drink from it, all of you. For this is my blood of the covenant, which is poured out for many for the forgiveness of sins.'"

Matthew 26:26-28

One of my daughters has a strange ailment that afflicts her every time she has her blood drawn. As soon as the needle goes into her arm, she passes out. The first time it happened, we were kind of surprised, but the next time it happened, we thought, "Hmmm, there she goes again." Now she's an adult, and it has continued to happen every time she gets her blood drawn. She will even pass out when she sees someone else getting their blood drawn, so we have to hand it to her: she is consistent, and she clearly does not have a medical career in her future.

I share this with you because I do understand that some of us are just a little squeamish when it comes to blood, so I promise there won't be any gory descriptions happening here. No one will need to pass out from anything you will read in the next few pages. But it's impossible to talk about the gospel without talking about the blood that Jesus poured out for us.

Anytime a message is about blood, I imagine a lot of people check out. It's much more palatable to share messages of love and laughter, of hope and healing. In our world today, it's so easy to come across messages that sound really good. They might even sound Christian because they're so heartwarming and reassuring. But when we read through Paul's letters to the early church, in virtually every letter we find that he issues warnings. Basically, he says that not everything we hear is going to be the truth (Romans 16:17-18; Galatians 1:8-9; 1 Timothy 6:3-5; 2 Timothy 2:16-18; Titus 1:6-16). For a long time, I moved past these sections in the Bible quickly because I wanted to get to the happier parts, or the parts I thought pertained more to me. But if Paul believed it was important to mention, it's important that we listen.

So, here we are, talking about blood and false messages. We're having a great time. I know. But please hang in there with me—because in our world today, especially in our social-media feeds and in online articles, we have messages coming at us all the time, and it can be challenging to distinguish what is true from what is partly true or mostly true. In my experience, there are four pseudo-gospels that are commonly shared in online Christian spaces.

Four Commonly Shared Pseudo-Gospels

The first is the *prosperity gospel*, which promotes a message of health and wealth for those who have enough faith. The prosperity gospel promises to deliver you to your own personal promised land where you will receive abundant material blessings, but this false gospel has nothing to offer the person who is hurting and suffering.

If we're not talking about the blood of Jesus, we're not talking about the gospel.

The second is the *progressive gospel,* which claims to hold a greater enlightenment about the Christian faith than that of prior generations. The progressive gospel portrays a version of Christianity that is more like an individual journey, unmoored from the traditions of historic Christianity, but when suffering strikes, the fluid nature of the progressive gospel cannot sustain a soul that desperately needs to be tethered to solid truth.

The third is the *positivity gospel,* which focuses on the parts of the Bible that make us feel good. The positivity gospel revels in a gospel of mercy and love, but it rarely mentions God's other attributes like truth and holiness. It is sometimes called moralistic therapeutic deism, which is sort of a mouthful. It peddles a message of positive self-talk, self-help, and self-determinism, and there is little room for the genuine lament of the sufferer when tragedy strikes close to home.

The fourth is the *popularity gospel,* which pours its time, energy, and resources into making Christianity look hip and cool. The popularity gospel is sometimes referred to as a seeker-sensitive model or an attractional-church model, because its main goal is to attract lots of people to come and check out how cool Jesus is, but again, when a crisis tears the fabric of one's life into pieces, the hurting soul needs something more than a polished production or impressive concert.

Over the years I have spent time swimming in all four of these "gospel" waters. I grew up in churches that were steeped in the prosperity gospel because that's where my family went to church. That was all I knew. In my young adult years, I attended a local church that I thought was far removed from the prosperity gospel that I grew up in, only to discover later that this new church was really immersed in the progressive gospel.

In the blogging world, I found a lovely cohort of Christian women writers, but I also noticed how large swaths of the online world lean heavily on the positivity gospel, wanting only to celebrate the more palatable parts of the Bible. And when I lived in Southern California, I saw firsthand how some churches were more interested in putting on an impressive production than preaching an old gospel with a bloody cross. In the end none of these four pseudo-gospels could offer my hurting soul what it needed.

But God, being rich in mercy, reached me with the truth of the gospel through his word. So, how can we tell if the message we're hearing is a pseudo-gospel or the real gospel? Well, we start by immersing ourselves in the truth of God's word, but there's also a telltale sign that will pretty quickly reveal if what we're hearing is a pseudo-gospel or the real thing.

The Telltale Sign

In a pseudo-gospel, people don't spend much time, if any time at all, talking about the blood that Jesus poured out on the cross for our sins. In fact, the words "blood" and "sin" will rarely come up because if they do, people will likely turn away. There's even a biblical precedent for this. On Day 13 we talked about the story in John 6 where Jesus took a small boy's lunch of five barley loaves and two fish and multiplied it to feed thousands of people. The next day that same crowd returned, presumably in want of more bread and fish, only this time Jesus wasn't serving a meal.

Jesus, knowing they have come for more food, moves his discussion from physical bread to spiritual bread. "I am the bread of life," Jesus tells them (John 6:35). Then he goes on to say, "The one who eats my flesh and drinks my blood has eternal life, and I will raise him up on the last day, because my flesh is true food and my blood is true drink" (v 54-55).

Needless to say, this message didn't go over as well as the distribution of free food the day before. The people grumbled and complained and "many of his disciples turned back and no longer accompanied him" (v 66). The crowds were large when the bread was free, but as soon as the message turned to Christ and his blood, many people turned away. People are no different today. But if we're not talking about the blood of Jesus, we're not talking about the gospel. I understand that talking about blood is not the easiest thing to do, especially when trying to reach a friend who is deeply immersed in one of the four pseudo-gospels, but it is the foundation of our faith.

Friends, if we are going to lead a quiet life—the kind that begins with a quiet heart—it's necessary that we take an inventory of the spaces we occupy—digitally, physically, spiritually, and relationally. If the influencers we follow online never talk about the fact that we're sinners in need of the grace that Christ purchased with his blood, then we must be cautious with how much influence we allow such people to have in our lives. The same is true of the churches we attend.

I don't write this to be downer or to be judgmental. Not at all. But there is a fire in my bones that the truth of God's word should be rightly proclaimed and that hurting souls will hear that no matter how desperate life gets, there is one who sees, there is one who knows, and there is one who has made a way through whatever situation feels so impossible at the moment.

Christ poured out his life so that we might live, and he offers his costly grace to us as a gift. And if there is one message we want to share with the world, it is this very good news. Indeed, it's the best news we could ever hear.

TUNING IN TO QUIET

Contemplate

1. Do you recognize any of the four pseudo-gospels in some of the posts in your social-media feed? Which ones, if any?
2. Why do you think some "Christian" influencers are reluctant to talk about the blood that Jesus poured out for our sins?
3. If you were to share the gospel of Jesus Christ with a friend, what would you say?

Cultivate

Just as we have been tuning our hearts to lead a quiet life, we must also tune our spirits to discern the true gospel from a false one. After contemplating the verses in today's reading, write down the basic tenets of the true gospel so you can quickly discern truth from error whenever you hear it, whether that's in online spaces or real-life places. And if you want some help on this, check out the resources at www.denisejhughes.com/gospel. Then talk with your pastor or spiritual mentor to confirm that you're clear about the gospel. Then ask God to show you one person in your life who needs to hear the gospel today.

Pray

Lord, the words "thank you" don't seem sufficient, but we have to tell you how grateful we are that you did not leave us to fend for ourselves in such a loud and noisy world that is constantly telling us messages that don't line up with your word. Thank you for the sacrifice you made on the cross.

Thank you for the blood you poured out for us. And thank you for the new life you give. We can only offer you our deepest praise for all of our days. In your loving name, Jesus, we pray. Amen.

Day 29

AFTER A LITTLE WHILE

"The God of all grace, who called you to his eternal glory in Christ, will himself restore, establish, strengthen, and support you after you have suffered a little while."

1 Peter 5:10

I mentioned earlier that I experienced complications from an abdominal surgery that resulted in multiple pulmonary embolisms. Obviously, I'm here, and I'm ok now. But there were moments when I didn't know if I would make it home from the hospital to see my kids grow up and have families of their own.

Lying in that hospital bed, I felt tangled in needles, tubes, and wires. I had two IVs, one in each arm, and I had these stickers all over my chest to monitor my elevated heart rate. Apparently, when the body has blood clots, the heart has to work extra hard to pump the blood, which can cause a heart attack or cardiac arrest. And since blood clots were floating around my body, a blood clot could have struck my brain at any moment and caused a stroke. I was in a pretty serious condition.

But while I was there, I tried to count my blessings, and one thing I was very grateful for was the fact that I had my own room with its own bathroom. I didn't have to worry about roommates and their visitors. This privacy was immensely helpful because it was impossible for me to get out of bed by myself. My abdomen hadn't yet healed from the surgery, so I needed help to sit up and get out of bed. At home my husband would have helped me, but in the hospital I needed the nurse's help.

Then, one morning in the hospital, on top of everything else, I started hemorrhaging in the bathroom. I called for the nurse, but she didn't come. I tried to mop up the mess, but the tangle of tubes and wires wouldn't let me bend over to reach the floor. The mess grew worse by the second.

About this time my heart monitor started blaring like a fire alarm. My nurse came running in and demanded I get back in bed. I tried to explain that I needed to clean up the mess, but she yelled over my protests, "You're going to have a heart attack if you don't get back in bed this instant!"

I obeyed.

After the nurse helped me back into bed, she walked over to the bathroom, took one look inside, closed the door, and flatly said, "I'll call housekeeping." Then she walked out of the room.

I wasn't sure what housekeeping could do. I was pretty sure only Moses could part the red sea in there, but later that hour a small woman, barely five feet (1.5m) tall, walked into my room. She had long black hair neatly coiled into a bun, and with a kind voice she said, "Hi. I'm housekeeping. I'm going to clean your room."

When she reached for the bathroom door, I said, "Wait! What's your name?"

She looked surprised and answered, "I'm Rosa."

I said, "Rosa, I am so sorry. I tried to clean it up, but I couldn't bend over, and I couldn't reach anything."

Rosa smiled and waved her hand as if to dismiss my concerns and said, "Oh, it's my pleasure."

She sounded like a Chick-Fil-A employee, but then she opened the bathroom door, took one look inside, closed the door, and walked out of my room. I thought to myself, "I don't blame you, Rosa. I don't blame you one bit."

But a few minutes later, Rosa came back. This time she wheeled in a cart behind her. Like a soldier going into battle, she put on plastic gloves that reached past her elbows. She wrapped each of her feet with little booties that looked like shower caps, and she placed a mask over her mouth and nose. With a mop and a gallon of bleach, Rosa stepped into my bathroom and closed the door behind her.

For the first time since being admitted to the hospital, the full weight of my situation bore down on me as it became painfully clear I couldn't fix anything. I couldn't fix my lungs. I couldn't fix my heart. I couldn't fix my blood, which was clotting against my will. I couldn't even clean up my own mess. I had never been so physically helpless in my entire life.

The smell of bleach filled my room, and when Rosa came out of the bathroom, she carried a large trash bag with her. I said, "Rosa, I am so sorry. I know it was awful in there."

Rosa looked at me, and with the same friendly voice she said again, "It's my pleasure." Then she pushed the cart out of my room.

I sat in bed stunned. Rosa went above and beyond her job that day. She could have huffed and puffed and shuffled about, making it clear that I had made her job much more difficult that day, but she didn't. Instead, she showed me kindness, and in doing so, she did more than clean up my mess—a mess I was incapable of cleaning on my own; she cleaned up my mess with grace.

That's what grace is: a gift of unwarranted kindness—freely given.

As I lay there and thought about the grace Rosa had shown me, I vowed in my heart that if I ever won the lottery, I would split my winnings with Rosa so she wouldn't have to clean hospital bathrooms anymore. But as soon as this idea entered my mind, I realized how even this sentiment was born of a desire on my part to pay her back for her kindness. I wanted to make it up to her so I could erase the debt I felt in my heart—as if such kindness could possibly have a dollar value attached! True grace is not only freely given; it's to be freely received, and to receive such grace is deeply humbling.

The Truth about Grace

In his letter to the Ephesians, the apostle Paul describes grace as a gift from God, and there is nothing we can do to earn it. He says, "For you are saved by grace through faith, and this is not from yourselves; it is God's gift—not from works, so that no one can boast" (2:8-9). In every human heart, a debt is owed that none of us can pay. We are sinners, and our sins, both individually and collectively, have made a horrible stinking mess that we cannot clean up on our own; yet Jesus steps into our mess, and he cleanses our hearts. He forgives us and wipes our slates clean. Then he turns to us and says, *It's my pleasure.* This is the good news of the gospel. Jesus did for us what we could not do for ourselves.

You and I may live in different places. We may have different stories and different life experiences. But one thing we all share is that we know what it's like to live in a world where there are deep disappointments and hurts. We know what it's like to struggle to breathe. Each of us will be walking through a different season right now, but if your heart has ever known the weight of a sorrow that is hard to put into words, I want you to know that God's grace is vast enough to cover everything. There is no mess too big and no circumstance too hard that God's grace cannot handle it.

God's grace is the reason why we can walk through each day with a quiet peace: because we know it's not up to us to fix our own messes. His mercy found us and made us new. So, we don't have to stress over the need to get ourselves cleaned up and made presentable. We don't have to feel anxious that people are going to judge us for not getting our act together. We just have to enter into God's presence and let him call us redeemed because the God of all grace promises that he himself will restore, establish, strengthen, and support us.

So, when we recognize our own inability to fix ourselves and we confidently rely on God to do the work in us instead, we can move through each day with genuine peace.

TUNING IN TO QUIET

Contemplate

1. What does 1 Peter 5:10 have to say about the timeframe for suffering? How might this truth bring comfort?
2. Can you think of a situation in your life when someone showed you grace? Or perhaps a time when you showed grace to someone else? What happened?
3. How would you describe God's grace to someone who is unfamiliar with this concept?

Cultivate

We've talked a lot about how the online social sphere is a noisy place, especially with so much self-promotion. But that doesn't mean digital spaces cannot be used for redemptive purposes. Today, tell the story of how the gospel of grace has changed you. Explain how God's grace did for you what you could not do for yourself. It doesn't have to be long, and it doesn't have to include a ton of personal details. But tell the story of how God and a bloody cross have given you a deep, abiding peace. The world desperately needs to hear of God's grace. Be a voice for his grace today.

Pray

Lord, we are in awe of the kindness you have shown us. We cannot ever fully know how much it cost you to give up your life for ours, but we bow our hearts to you in adoration. We thank you and praise you that nothing is too hard for you. No mess is too big for you. We can come to you in utter brokenness, and you offer us wholeness. What a good God you are! We love you, Lord. In your grace-filled name, Jesus, we pray. Amen.

Day 30

A SANCTUARY OF PRAISE

"Praise God in his sanctuary. Praise him in his mighty expanse."

Psalm 150:1

I have a secret. Well, it's not really a secret, but it's something I do quietly during the five months or so it takes to write a book. Since there are 150 psalms in the Psalter and there are about 150 days in a five-month period, I read a psalm each day before I write. The psalms are full of highs and lows, with mountaintop praises and valley laments, and every book-making venture is similarly filled with normal ups and downs. Actually, this is true about life in general, whether someone is writing a book or not, which is why the psalms are always a great place for us to go. They remind us that joy and grief and everything in between are human experiences common to all.

After reading through 149 psalms, the final psalm is a fitting call for everyone to praise God in the sanctuary. What better way to finish any journey than with praise?

A Plan for Praise

The anonymous writer of this psalm offers a succinct yet comprehensive plan, if you will, for praise. In effect, he covers the six journalistic questions—the five W's and one H: *Who? What? When? Where? Why? How?*

What are we called to do? Praise the Lord (Psalm 150:1). *Where* are we to praise him? In the sanctuary (v 1). *Why* should we praise him? For his powerful acts, according to his abundant greatness (v 2). *How* should we praise him? With the blast of a horn, with harp and lyre, with tambourine and dance and, yes, with loud "clashing cymbals" (v 3-5). Because not all loud sounds are noise! Some loud sounds are joyous expressions of great love and deep gladness and overwhelming gratitude. And *who* should praise him? Everything that breathes (v 6).

That final command in the last sentence of the psalter is especially poignant for me. I know what it is to labor for every breath, to fight against impaired lungs to draw in the faintest gasp of much-needed oxygen. And yet, as long as any of us have breath, we are to praise the Lord. In the sanctuary. In the hospital. In the home. In the workplace. In the neighborhood. In the marketplace. And in digital spaces, too. Wherever we are, we are to praise him.

As much as I have shared my concerns—and I have many—regarding the loud, vacuous noise that fills so many digital dwellings, I hope I have also communicated that not everyone will be called to withdraw completely from online realms. Rather, whatever metaspaces we occupy, we want to do so with a heart that wants to bring praise to God and not to ourselves.

Lastly, in Psalm 150 we're left with one question: *When* are we to praise him? The psalmist doesn't explicitly state the answer in the text, but we can surmise, based on everything in the psalms, that we are to praise the Lord at all times for

Praise is the language of a hope-filled soul.

all eternity. This is also evidenced by the glimpse we're given into that heavenly sanctuary, where four living creatures are stationed around the throne, never ceasing to say, "Holy, holy, holy, Lord God, the Almighty, who was, who is, and who is to come" (Revelation 4:8).

Praise is what we find in the sanctuary, and it's the language of a hope-filled soul.

From Praise to Peace

In response to all the noise and worldly messages we hear, we long for a place where the chaos of our daily lives is supplanted with a peace that cannot be described. We long for peace. But true peace can only be found in God's sanctuary. In the Old Testament, the sanctuary was a place only a priest could enter. Now all believers are a royal priesthood, who can enter God's presence with confidence because Christ poured out his blood as the ultimate once-and-for-all sacrifice to pay the ransom for our sins.

Today, the places in which God's people meet, often called "sanctuaries," can look vastly different. Some are cathedrals adorned with brilliant stained-glass windows and elaborate architecture. Some are simple steeple-topped brick buildings with a center aisle dividing two rows of wooden pews. Some are extensive big-box spaces made with cement cinderblocks and filled with theater-style seating. And then some congregations don't have a designated place to worship at all, so they gather in school cafeterias or gymnasiums. Still others prefer to meet inside someone's home.

Wherever God's people choose to gather, every sanctuary bears the unique imprint of its local fellowship. Some will place the Lord's table front and center to signify the importance of communion among the saints. Some will feature a baptistery in a prominent place, to communicate the significance of this sacrament in a believer's life. Some will place the podium to the side of the platform, leaving a large cross as the central focal point, to remind the worshippers of the preeminence of Christ's work on the cross. And then some will have a variety of staging and lighting effects.

The main purpose, however, for every Christ-centered church is to gather and worship Christ. This is the invitation to the sanctuary for you today. Whatever you have been through. Whatever you are going through right now. And whatever you may go through someday. Will you bring your hurts to a world that can only offer a pseudo-solution? Or will you bring your hurts into the presence of Christ?

His sanctuary is open to you because his poured-out blood has made entrance into his presence possible. It's really the only place on earth where true peace can be found, and the only appropriate response is to give God all the praise for all glory belongs to him.

TUNING IN TO QUIET

Contemplate

1. What is the primary command in Psalm 150:1? How can you personally fulfill this command?
2. No matter what our current circumstances might be, why do we always have reason to give God praise?
3. Why are shouts of praise considered congruent with leading a quiet life?

Cultivate

Just as God is with you wherever you go, you can also praise him wherever you go. And yet, something special always happens when God's people come together to praise him in unity. That's one of the reasons why corporate worship is so important. It's a chance for us to gather, and in unity we can lift our voices in praise. To be a part of such expressions of unity buoys the heart. Today, lift up your voice in a shout of praise. Yes, I said *shout*.

Pray

Lord, thank you for the standing invitation you offer for all to come into your sanctuary. Thank you for making a way possible for us to enter your presence. Thank you for the peace you alone can give. In you alone our hearts find rest from a noisy and demanding world. And to you we lift up our voices in the loudest shouts of praise. We love you, Lord, with our whole being. In your worthy name, Jesus, we pray. Amen.

Day 31

A NEW SOJOURN BEGINS

"Not that I have already reached the goal or am already perfect, but I make every effort to take hold of it because I also have been taken hold of by Christ."

Philippians 3:12

For one year in high school, I was—most regrettably—a cheerleader. My brief career as a megaphone-shouting encourager began the summer my squad attended cheer camp at Stanford University. We stayed in the dorms along with 600 other cheerleaders, and everyone wore their uniforms with their high-school mascot stitched somewhere on their vest or sweater. This wasn't a problem if your team's mascot was derived from a name like the Bears or Tigers or Colts. But our mascot? We were the Honkers. Yep, our town's pride was embroidered in bright gold letters right across our chests: HONKERS.

Naturally, the other cheerleaders at camp would ask us, "What's a honker?" So, we'd explain that a honker is a Canada goose. Our hometown has a wildlife refuge—sort of like a sanctuary—just outside the city limits, and every year thousands of Canada geese fill the sky as they migrate to our town for the winter. They're quite elegant looking, too, with their long, sleek black necks and their curvy white cheeks, but as soon as they open their beaks, all bets are off. They make a rather loud, obnoxious sound that can only be described as a honk—hence, their nickname. A part of me secretly wished we could have been the Eagles or Falcons or Seahawks, but, alas, I spent that part of my youth chanting, "Go, Honkers, go!"

After high school, I was glad to leave my honking days behind me. I wanted something quieter, more sophisticated, maybe even demure. But the world has only gotten louder around me. With the megaphone that the internet has become, most of the North American continent has become a hemisphere of honkers. Between Twitter wars, social-media shaming, and constant self-promotion, the noise has reached deafening levels.

Most of us are doing the best we can in this "brave new world"—as it was dubbed by the author Aldous Huxley—but we also recognize the inherent value in charting a different journey than the one the world beckons us to follow. This journey isn't to an idealistic past or an alternative utopian future. Rather, travelers on this journey look both backward and forward. We look back on the tabernacle-sanctuary, learning what it stood for and whom it pointed toward, and we look forward to that heavenly sanctuary where we will one day be in the very presence of God. We also look to ways in which we can cultivate a sanctuary of the heart right here and now, making it our ambition to lead a quiet life.

Honkers and Saints

In recent days, I have found myself back at high-school football games because one of my daughters is on the high-school varsity dance team. At her first game, my husband and I sat on the metal bleachers to watch our girl perform with metallic gold

To cultivate a quiet heart isn't a one-time act or a one-stop journey. It's an ongoing habit of grace.

pom-poms. Then at one point, all the girls in uniform started chanting, "Go, Saints, go!"

Saints. That's their mascot. Isn't that so much better? Wouldn't we all rather be a Saint than a Honker? The world today is filled with far too many honkers. We could use a few more saints—saints who cultivate a quiet heart.

In every one of Paul's letters, his opening words address the saints because the church is made up of the saints, since those who put their faith in Christ are called such. That includes you and me. If we could summarize all of Paul's letters in three words, it might be this: *Go, saints, go!*

That's what I want us to hear, too. As you have already begun this journey toward cultivating a quiet heart, keep going. Never give up. Finish strong. It's worth it!

I don't know about you, but I don't ever want to sound like a Honker. I've already been there, done that. Whenever my high-school football team scored a touchdown, somehow it was my job to retrieve the one Canada goose we had in a crate. I would hold the goose by its two legs above my head and run the length of the football field while the goose flapped its wings and honked.

Thankfully, my days of running with honkers are over. Not because I've reached some ultimate destination but because I know I'm heading in the right direction. My prayer for you is the same: that this sojourn doesn't end with these 31 days but that it's really just beginning. To cultivate a quiet heart isn't a one-time act or a one-stop journey. It's an ongoing habit of grace. Seeking God first. Knowing that when we seek him, we find him when we seek him with all of our heart (Jeremiah 29:13).

Go, saints, go!

TUNING IN TO QUIET

Contemplate

1. Why is it important to look back at the tabernacle-sanctuary in the Bible and learn the ways in which it pointed toward Christ?
2. Why is it important to look ahead to that heavenly sanctuary where we will one day be in the presence of God?
3. Why is it important to cultivate a quiet sanctuary of the heart, right here and now?

Cultivate

The funny thing about leading a quiet life is that you don't need ecstatic cheerleaders or pump-you-up encouragement from Instagram squares because once you're living from a place of quiet confidence, your motivation comes from within. As you walk in step with the Holy Spirit, you quietly look to God in his word for encouragement, not to the many voices with selfies on social media. And what you find in God is real because his word speaks life. Now you are becoming the person others look to. They see the difference in you. You are walking differently. You are talking differently. Because you are living differently. Not that you have already attained any level of perfection. But you are moving in a different direction. And the world takes notice. Today, I want to encourage you to keep going. Keep your eyes fixed on Christ. Go, saint, go!

Pray

Lord, we are in awe that before time began you had a plan, and your plan included your children—sons and daughters whom you know by name. When you chose your children as your own, you conferred an identity on each and every one. You called us out of darkness and into your light. You called us saints, the "called out ones," and you said we are your beloved. There is no greater blessing or privilege than to be loved by you. Thank you for loving us and calling us your own. Thank you for providing a way for us to enter into your sanctuary, into your presence. Help us to live each day with a quiet heart and a quiet confidence, knowing that one day we will live eternally in your presence. In your wonderful name, Jesus, we pray all these things, Amen.

Afterword

A BLESSING FOR YOUR JOURNEY

"May the LORD bless you and protect you; may the LORD make his face shine on you and be gracious to you; may the LORD look with favor on you and give you peace."

Numbers 6:24-26

Cultivating a quiet heart isn't something we do one time and then move on to something else. It's an ongoing journey, a daily working out of what Christ has worked in us. Then, as we grow more and more into Christ's likeness, we become a light to those around us. We become witnesses to his goodness, truth, and beauty. So, with each new day we're given, let us remember to…

1. Acknowledge those things we rely on more than God and ask for his forgiveness.
2. Reduce some of the external noise in our lives by giving up one online activity.
3. Fill that open space daily with the truth of God's word.
4. Ask God to give us a one-thing heart.
5. Invite a trusted friend to walk alongside us as we cultivate a quiet life.

6. Slip outside to admire either the sunset or the sunrise and thank God for the light he brings into darkness.
7. Set aside a consistent bedtime and remember who the real provider and sustainer is.
8. Identify a person who needs a friend and reach out to be that friend.
9. Bring our hurts and sorrows to God instead of the digital world.
10. Place three encouraging Bible verses either on our phone via the Notes App or on an index card.
11. Make a casserole—or something else you enjoy—and deliver a meal to a friend in need.
12. Offer the work of our hands as a blessing to someone.
13. Serve in small ways and remember that nothing is small in God's eyes.
14. Submit to God's word as the ultimate authority in our life.
15. Welcome the Holy Spirit's conviction as a means of grace.
16. Put away our phone to love others with our intentional focus and physical presence.
17. Keep an eternal perspective by seeing the things around us as temporary.
18. Practice generosity by giving away something we enjoy.
19. Let God define us and loss refine us.
20. Write out our questions and doubts in a prayer journal.

21. Give thanks to God for being with us wherever we go.
22. Embrace the habit of gathering regularly with God's people.
23. Take a sound inventory and create times of actual quiet.
24. Select the sources, both in online spaces and real-life places, worthy of our focus.
25. Find an older saint whose life we would want to emulate.
26. Prioritize the places we're in and the people we're with over digital connections.
27. Savor the beauty of God's creation.
28. List the basic tenets of the gospel so we can discern truth from error.
29. Tell the story of how the gospel of grace has changed us.
30. Lift up our voice in a shout of praise to God.
31. Continue to cultivate a quiet life each day by keeping our eyes on Christ.

You won't always get everything right, and neither will I. Sometimes we will falter and fail. But when we confess our sins, God is faithful to forgive us and grant us a new start. This is why he says his mercies are new every morning (Lamentations 3:22-23, NIV). Every day is another opportunity for us to be living testimonies to the peace we find in Christ as our sanctuary. To God be all the glory.

Endnotes

1 Charles Spurgeon, "A Little Sanctuary," http://www.spurgeongems.org/sermon/chs2001.pdf (accessed April 23, 2021).

2 Chris Bail, *Breaking the Social Media Prism: How to Make Our Platforms Less Polarizing* (Princeton University Press, 2021), p 53.

3 https://medium.com/@rachel_hall/why-kids-want-to-be-youtubers-when-they-grow-up-4d7a4074b44

4 Warren W. Wiersbe, *Be Delivered: Finding Freedom by Following God* (David C. Cook, 1998), p 170.

5 Kate Battistelli, "The Bronze Mirror," CSB (in)courage Devotional Bible (Holman Bible Publishers, 2018), p 142.

6 Tony Merida, *Christ-Centered Exposition: Exalting Jesus in Exodus* (B&H Publishing Group, 2014), p 170.

7 https://biblehub.com/interlinear/1_thessalonians/4.htm (accessed May 17, 2022).

8 Jen Pollock Michel, *Teach Us to Want: Longing, Ambition, and the Life of Faith* (IVP Books, 2014), p 24.

9 Jen Pollock Michel, p 42.

10 https://www.nytimes.com/2020/04/28/technology/digital-influencers-coronavirus.html

11 R.C. Sproul, *The Holiness of God*, chapter 2.

12 C.S. Lewis, *The Weight of Glory* (Harper One, 1949), p 40-41.

13 *Shekinah* is a term used in the Old Testament to depict the glory of God's divine presence. It is usually represented as a brilliant light.

14 Jay Kim, *Analog Church: Why We Need Real People, Places, and Things in the Digital Age* (IVP Books, 2020), p 108-109.

15 Warren W. Wiersbe, *Be Holy: Becoming "Set Apart" for God* (David C. Cook, 1994), p 140.

16 Allan Moseley, *Christ-Centered Exposition: Exalting Jesus in Leviticus* (B&H Publishing Group, 2015), p 221.

BIBLICAL | RELEVANT | ACCESSIBLE

At The Good Book Company, we are dedicated to helping Christians and local churches grow. We believe that God's growth process always starts with hearing clearly what he has said to us through his timeless word—the Bible.

Ever since we opened our doors in 1991, we have been striving to produce Bible-based resources that bring glory to God. We have grown to become an international provider of user-friendly resources to the Christian community, with believers of all backgrounds and denominations using our books, Bible studies, devotionals, evangelistic resources, and DVD-based courses.

We want to equip ordinary Christians to live for Christ day by day, and churches to grow in their knowledge of God, their love for one another, and the effectiveness of their outreach.

Call us for a discussion of your needs or visit one of our local websites for more information on the resources and services we provide.

Your friends at The Good Book Company